1c-Ref-A- NLS-17.50

STOP
THE PRESSES!

STOP THE PRESSES!

THE NEWSPAPERMAN IN AMERICAN FILMS

ALEX BARRIS

SOUTH BRUNSWICK AND NEW YORK: A. S. BARNES AND COMPANY
LONDON: THOMAS YOSELOFF LTD

A.S. Barnes and Co., Inc.
Cranbury, New Jersey 08512

Thomas Yoseloff Ltd
108 New Bond Street
London W1Y OQX, England

Library of Congress Cataloging in Publication Data

Barris, Alex.
Stop the presses!

Includes index.
1. Journalists in motion-pictures.   2.   Moving-
pictures—United States.   I. Title.
PN1995.9.J6B3   791.43'0909'352   74-30718
ISBN 0-498-01603-X

PRINTED IN THE UNITED STATES OF AMERICA

To newspaper people everywhere,
but especially in Toronto

CONTENTS

STOP
THE PRESSES!

1
THE PROTOTYPE

In Billy Wilder's 1950 film, *Sunset Boulevard,* there's a scene in which Gloria Swanson, as the aging silent-movie star yearning for a comeback, screens some of her vintage epics for William Holden, whose aid she hopes to enlist. Carried away by her own celluloid image, she stands dramatically and praises the good old silent days, when "we didn't need words."

That notion is one that silent film buffs cling to tenaciously, somewhat in defiance of the facts. What Charlie Chaplin, D.W. Griffith, and other creative men of the silent era did — and often superbly — was try to compensate for the inescapable fact that there was as yet no technique for producing sound on film, no way for actors to be *heard* speaking while they were *seen* speaking.

This was not, in the first place, pure mime of the sort developed by the *commedia dell'arte* which relied intentionally on the ability of actors to tell a story by using gestures and facial expressions, the kind of mime represented today by Marcel Marceau. This was, in fact, make-do mime, necessitated by the absence of any effective way of presenting audible dialogue along with the visual action.

Admittedly, the silent screen geniuses achieved wonders in overcoming this problem, especially in the development of visual comedy and "action" films, and nothing said here is intended to diminish their considerable accomplishments.

Nevertheless, the silent screen did have to cheat, very often, in getting across some of the finer points of a story. The use of title cards, on which key words of dialogue were printed, was the best they could do when actions (and the lack of the spoken word) failed them.

Beyond the argument that title cards cheated in the art of pure mime is the more pertinent one that those necessary but intrusive cards often succeeded only in destroying the pace and rhythm of the director's work, serving to slow down the action rather than build up suspense.

The artistry of silent film directors and actors was in their ability to convey any sort of progression of story ideas when they were so hampered by the absence of sound. To insist that silent cinema was somehow "better," or that film "lost its art" when it found its voice is hardly defensible.

Not long after the novelty of the hair-raising chase and the pie in the face began to wear thin, silent-film producers sought to upgrade the quality of cinema by translating "great plays" to the screen. Quaint though it now may seem, even such classics as *Romeo and Juliet, Othello,* and *Hamlet* were filmed (and more than once) as silent movies. One wonders if the rationale that "we didn't need words" was regarded as applicable to the works of Shakespeare, Dumas, Tolstoy, or Shaw.

Whatever the merits of the silent cinema artists — and they have been handsomely heralded by numerous historians of the era — it is doubtful that cinema would have become the worldwide force in communications it has if sound films had never been perfected.

The movie-going public was certainly ready

for sound by the time it came along. In 1927, the last year dominated by silent films (sound was tried out on the public in October of that year), the weekly movie-theater attendance across the United States was fifty-seven million. By the end of 1929, when most theaters were equipped to show sound films, the weekly attendance had leaped by some forty percent, to ninety-five million. And despite the stock-market crash late that year and the ensuing Great Depression, the figures never slipped back to anything like the presound attendance. In the decade between 1930 and 1939, the weekly attendance figures averaged out at seventy-six million.

Mime, gestures, and title cards sufficed for a while in telling stories, but very often the essence of a story even slightly more complex than boy-meets-girl or cops-catch-robbers had to be sacrificed by the limitations of speechlessness. The introduction of sound to film liberated writers, directors, and actors from the severe strictures of story-telling via pictures, and quite often grotesquely exaggerated gestures.

More than that, it added a missing dimension to film story-telling — the one that was initially regarded as vital when plays and novels were devised: people talking.

Nowhere was this more welcome than in the Hollywood light comedies that began to fill the screen, and delight audiences, from the introduction of sound onward. However "unrealistic" (i.e., glamorous) these comedies about love and marriage and flirtations and foolish misunderstandings may have been, they were accepted by the mass audience as being more like life than the inspired antics of Chaplin and Keaton, the mad chases of Keystone Cops, or the cliff-hanging escapades of Douglas Fairbanks.

Like all popular fiction, of course, these new talking romantic comedies were larger than life, the heroes wittier than you or I, the heroines more elaborately decked out, the complications more imaginative. But at least superficially it was easier to accept actors and actresses who could be heard talking as "real" human beings, characters an audience could more or less relate to.

In certain types of movies, the dialogue was absolutely essential to the effective telling of a story. If it was not as important (nor as interesting) in westerns, action stories, and spectacles, it was that much more important in "modern" (at the time) comedies, stories of crime detection, and, obviously, musicals.

One other type of movie that could hardly have developed into the Hollywood staple that it became had it not been for the addition of sound was the newspaper story. If there was ever any great (or even reasonably entertaining) silent newspaper movie it fails to come to mind.

Yet, almost from the beginning of the talking era, the newspaperman has been a recognizable movie type, characterized by his wise-cracking, his insulting manner toward his bosses, and his breezy irreverence to editors, politicians, police, advertisers, publicity seekers, and female reporters. All these traits could be far more successfully conveyed through that missing ingredient in silent films: dialogue.

Writers at work: Charles MacArthur (seated) and Ben Hecht, two former newsmen who virtually immortalized the American reporter in their play *The Front Page.*

12

Of course, it was no more true that all reporters were witty or fearless or cynical than that all cowboys were heroic or that all villains wore black hats or that all policemen were as funny as the Keystone Cops. These were badges, costumes, symbols by which characters were recognized and accepted by the movie-going public.

Ben Hecht and Charles MacArthur may not have invented the movie newspaperman, but they were largely responsible for his proliferation and longevity. In the same year that talking pictures were starting to sweep the country (1928), the Messrs. Hecht and MacArthur concocted *The Front Page,* a play that was not only one of the big hits of that Broadway season but was to become the yardstick by which

virtually all newspaper movies for the next several decades would be measured.

Unlike so many of the movies that it helped to spawn, *The Front Page* did not take place in a newspaper office. All the action in the three-act play was set in one place, the press room of the Criminal Courts Building in Chicago. Here, an assortment of cynical, glib, jaded newspapermen for various (fictional) Chicago papers waited for the moment when a convicted murderer was to be hanged.

The principal characters are Hildy Johnson, of the *Herald Examiner,* played in that first production by Lee Tracy, and his editor, Walter Burns, played by Osgood Perkins. The original cast, incidentally, also included such supporting actors as Allen Jenkins, George

The Front Page. Walter Burns (Adolphe Menjou) is the image of injured innocence in this scene. But Hildy Johnson (Pat O'Brien, at right) knows him better. (United Artists, 1931)

Barbier, Willard Robertson, Joseph Calleia, and Eduardo Cianelli, all of whom subsequently became known to movie buffs.

Hildy, fed up with the newspaper business in general and the unrelenting demands of his boss in particular, is about to quit, marry a sweet young thing, and defect to New York and an advertising-agency job. (That is one of the recurring daydreams of most newspapermen; the other is about settling down in some small town and running a weekly.) But Walter Burns is determined not to lose his ace reporter.

The Front Page. Mae Clark is ready to take on all the pressroom regulars in this scene. She played a prostitute who loved the condemned man. (United Artists, 1931)

When the condemned murderer escapes and blunders into the press room, where Hildy is temporarily alone, the magnet of an exclusive story is too much for Hildy to resist. He hides the terrified little man inside a roll-top desk and plots frantically to scoop the opposition.

What made *The Front Page* such a smash hit was clearly not its plot but its outrageous characters. Hildy and his colleagues are pictured as cynics to whom the life or death of a man is of far less consequence than whether the life or death will be determined in time to meet a deadline.

Yet, Hecht and MacArthur contrived to make these hard-boiled cynics seem human and, above all, amusing. They drink, play cards to stave off boredom, insult each other, tell tall tales, show an irresistible lack of respect for all public officials, alibi for each other's absences (as when an irate wife is searching for an errant husband), and, most of all, hate their editors with a burning passion.

The character of Walter Burns was supposedly based on a man named Walter Howie who had been city editor of a Chicago paper for which Hecht had worked in his own newspaper days. Howie had a glass eye, and Hecht has been quoted as saying it was easy to tell which was the glass eye — it was the warmer one.

Next to the fanatic hatred for editors, the quality most common to the Hecht-MacArthur reporters was the kind of dedication to duty that would make D'Artagnan seem like a shirker. Audiences were asked to believe — and obviously did believe — that despite all the dirty tricks Walter Burns had played on him, despite his resolve to quit, to marry the girl, to flee to New York, Hildy Johnson would be riveted to his job by the prospect of an exclusive story, a scoop. It's the kind of mystical devotion to a higher purpose than self-interest that actors profess (and audiences expect them to) in observing the traditional dictum that no matter what other considerations have to be discarded, The Show Must Go On.

Thus, it became part of the mythology about American newspaper reporters that The Story was always their prime consideration, that to get The Story, any means were justified, any deceit pardonable, any extreme understandable. Editors, naturally, felt the same way, even adding one more touch of fanaticism: any number of hours worked by a reporter in pursuit of The Story should be regarded as being in the line of duty.

There was, indeed, a kernel of truth in all this. Loyalty to one's work is admirable in any field of endeavor, and its existence among journalists was probably at least as common as, say, among good soldiers or dauntless used-car salesmen.

Fiction, however, is not so much a reflection of life as a distillation of its more bizarre elements. Comedy is rooted in exaggeration. Thus, if a real-life reporter would grudgingly miss a meal to meet a deadline, a fictional one must sacrifice his romance or marriage rather than miss a scoop. If a real editor was businesslike and aloof a fictional one must be little short of a heartless despot. And if real-life politicians or police were sometimes pompous or slow, fictional ones must be charlatans or bungling idiots.

There were some newspaper movies before *The Front Page,* including such silents as *The Star Reporter* (1921), *Headlines* (1925), *Freedom of the Press,* and *Telling the World* (both 1928), the last-named starring William Haines. Among the early talkies dealing with the press were *Gentlemen of the Press* (1929),

with Walter Huston; *Big News* (1929), in which Robert Armstrong and Carole Lombard were rival reporters; and *Night Ride* (1929), with reporter Joseph Schildkraut getting the better of gangster Edward G. Robinson. In 1930, Norman Foster was a sports writer and Claudette Colbert a gossip columnist in *Young Man of Manhattan.*

While these and other early movies about the newspaper business captured some of the atmosphere of big-city journalism and suggested some of the characteristics by which audiences could identify newspapermen, they tended generally to lean more on melodrama and less on comedy, more on the clashes between newspapermen and their quarry than between reporters and their editors. What *The*

Telling the World. William Haines is the natty reporter trying to sweet talk the boss's secretary in this, one of the last silent films about the press. (MGM, 1928)

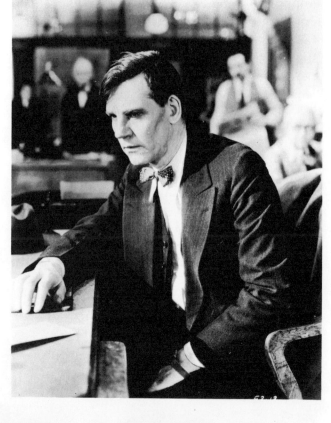

Big News. Carole Lombard and Robert Armstrong were both newshounds, working on rival papers. (Pathé, 1929)

Gentlemen of the Press. Walter Huston is the troubled-looking newsman mulling over some journalistic decision. (Paramount, 1929)

Night Ride. Reporter Joseph Schildkraut (center) barely survived the one-way ride in this melodrama. (Universal, 1929)

Front Page did was to reduce the story (the impending execution of a convicted killer and his subsequent escape and recapture) to a secondary position, focusing instead on the continuing conflict between Hildy Johnson and Walter Burns, a far less significant but infinitely more entertaining theme.

A couple of years after *The Front Page* became a stage hit, another play, called *Five Star Final,* was produced on Broadway. Written by Louis Weitzenkorn, it was an expose of the depths to which yellow journalism could descend. In *Five Star Final,* the executives of a New York tabloid goad the managing editor into digging up an old scandal that destroys the lives of several innocent people — and all merely to boost the paper's failing circulation. It was stark, effective melodrama, but almost totally lacking in the kind of humor that Hecht and MacArthur had found as a redeeming feature of the journalistic jungle.

Five Star Final was nevertheless a Broadway success and beat *The Front Page* to the screen by a couple of months. Both plays became films in 1931 and both were well received. The movie version of *Five Star Final* had Edward G. Robinson as the tough managing editor and a supporting cast that included H.B. Warner, Aline MacMahon, Frances Starr, and, in the role of a creepy newspaperman, Boris Karloff.

The Front Page was filmed with Pat

The newsroom. A familiar scene to movie fans was this center of activity in hundreds of newspaper movies. The editor wearing the eye shade is Charles Wilson, who played many editor roles.

O'Brien as Hildy Johnson and Adolphe Menjou as Walter Burns. Among the supporting newspapermen were Edward Everett Horton, Walter Catlett, and Frank McHugh. George E. Stone was the pathetic killer, and Mae Clarke played the prostitute who loved him.

Of the two films, *The Front Page* was predictably much the better and seems far less dated today than *Five Star Final*. The following spring, when Academy Awards time rolled around, *The Front Page* was nominated for best picture of the year, Menjou was nominated as best actor, and Lewis Milestone, who directed the picture, was also nominated in his category. That none of these nominations blossomed into awards was neither more nor less a freak of luck than has oftentimes since been witnessed by disappointed followers of Oscar-selecting.

But *The Front Page* accomplished something much more significant: it set a pattern that was to be used again and again, followed, imitated, distorted, sometimes equaled, and occasionally improved upon. In all the bumpy history of Hollywood, nothing has been more evident than that blind adherence to the philosophy of Me-Tooism that leads producers to believe that if one man can turn out a successful movie on a given theme, then anyone can achieve equal success merely by copying the original. The remarkable thing is how often audiences will sit still for this sort of shabby treatment.

Certainly, audiences accepted the image of the newspaper reporter projected by these early films — both the Hecht-MacArthur version of a witty, irreverent, but essentially likable guy, and the more melodramatic image of the unfeeling muckraker or the fearless crime solver.

Real-life newspapermen, it is true, tended at first to ridicule this image of tarnished glamour that movies about reporters sketched of them. In time, some of them began to chafe uncomfortably at the distortions, and often those among them who were charged with reviewing films could not resist applying the incisive (if not totally objective) standards of the expert witness in assessing the rather spurious evidence on the screen.

This was an advantage, and perhaps an unfair one, that no other group of viewers could utilize effectively in judging films. It may have been unfair because the yardstick of their own image of themselves was, at best, often irrelevant.

To illustrate the point, the 1955 film *Marty*, written by Paddy Chayefsky, was widely regarded as an honest, unpretentious story about a lonely Bronx butcher who grasps at a last chance to find love and happiness. It was thus accepted by millions of moviegoers and it was suitably honored at Academy Awards time. But it is almost a certainty that some living butchers viewed it as a terribly phony movie on the flimsy grounds that Ernest Borgnine, in the title role, didn't know how to hold a meat cleaver.

Similarly, when *Zorba the Greek* was being hailed as a great film, many Americans of Greek descent squirmed uncomfortably and mumbled objections about the movie's distortions of Greek character. Movies about doctors are often ludicrous (if not infuriating) to doctors; lawyers wince at the courtroom antics of screen lawyers; the residents of a Texas town were up in arms at the unfavorable light in which Larry McMurtry showed them in *The Last Picture Show*. Only Arthur Miller was shrewd enough, in creating Willy Loman in (*Death of a Salesman*) to purposely leave undefined exactly what it was that Willy was engaged in selling — thus denying millions of salesmen of specific articles the unction of either disassociating themselves from Miller's sweeping condemnations or pointing out minuscule technical inaccuracies.

The irony of all this, when brought back to the subject of newspapermen, is that while the butchers could comfort themselves with the argument that Chayefsky didn't know anything about pork chops, the Texans and the Greeks could fall back on standard defenses about Hollywood distortions, the newspapermen had nowhere to go: their movie image was invented by their own erstwhile colleagues.

Ben Hecht and Charles MacArthur had both been Chicago newspapermen in good standing before they turned playwrights. Louis Weitzenkorn, who wrote *Five Star Final*, had been a New York newspaper

18

editor. *Gentlemen of the Press,* with Walter Huston, was based on a play by Ward Morehouse, another journalist. The screenplay of *Young Man of Manhattan* was by yet another former newspaperman, Robert Presnell. Both in the beginning and in the decades of movies to follow, former newspapermen played a large part in molding and perpetuating that romantically magnified image of reporters and editors that made real newsmen cringe as often as it made audiences laugh.

Hecht, who spent many years in Hollywood, was later responsible for *Nothing Sacred,* a deliciously wry look at journalistic cynicism, and *Comrade X,* which dealt with the comic exploits of a foreign correspondent in Russia. And many years later, another Hecht story, called *Gaily, Gaily,* was turned into a lively movie about the misadventures of a young newspaperman in Chicago.

Even before talking pictures began, the Hollywood writing community included a number of former newspapermen, and from the beginning of the sound era, more and more of them flocked to the West Coast to write movie scripts.

Many of them, of course, wrote numerous scripts that had nothing to do with newspapers. But it is instructive to trace how many former journalists were at least partly responsbile (to the extent that any screen writer can be considered responsible for the final version of any film) for so many movies involving reporters, columnists, editors, publishers, and sob sisters.

Among the early ones in Hollywood was the legendary Herman J. Mankiewicz, a graduate of the Hearst newspaper empire, who topped his career by writing *Citizen Kane,* one of the most incisive of all newspaper movies and also one of the most stimulating films ever made in America. His screen credits also include a 1935 newspaper movie, *After Office Hours.*

Herman's younger brother, Joseph L. Mankiewicz, was involved in the production of several films that dealt, to some degree or other, with newspaper people, among them *Love on the Run, The Philadelphia Story, Woman of the Year, and All About Eve.* Like Herman, Joe also started out as a newspaper writer. (Many years later, Don Mankiewicz,

one of Herman's sons, wrote the screenplay for *I Want To Live,* in which a newspaper reporter was a key character.)

Allen Rivkin, once a Minneapolis newspaperman, wrote (alone or as collaborator) the screenplays for such newspaper-oriented movies as *Is My Face Red* (1932), *Headline Shooters* (1934), *Picture Snatcher* (1933), and *Behind the News* (1940).

Roy Chanslor, another journalist in his earlier days, supplied Hollywood with such material as *The Final Edition* (1932), *Hi, Nellie* (1934), *Front Page Woman* (1935), *The Girl on the Front Page* (1936), and a few others.

Samuel Fuller, who had worked on newspapers in New York and San Diego, has been involved (as screenwriter, producer, and/or director) with such newspaper films as *Confirm or Deny* (1941), *Park Row* and *Scandal Sheet* (both in 1952), and *Shock Corridor* (1963).

Rian James, once a *Brooklyn Eagle* columnist and later a foreign correspondent, had a hand in writing such newspaper movies as *Love Is a Racket* (1932), *We're Only Human* (1936), and *Exclusive* (1937).

Art Arthur, another *Brooklyn Eagle* alumnus (although originally from Toronto), whose versatile typewriter could swing from Charlie Chan mysteries to Ritz Brothers comedies to Lloyd Bridges underwater adventures, managed to sneak in a few newspaper scripts, too, among them *Love and Hisses* (1938) and *Everything Happens at Night* (1939).

Claude Binyon, who was later to become a top director, started as a Chicago newsman and wrote for the screen such successful films as *The Gilded Lily* and *The Bride Comes Home* (both in 1935), which involved newspapermen in leading roles.

The list is, if not endless, both impressive and varied. It includes such respected Hollywood names as Nunnally Johnson (*Roxie Hart,* 1942), Dudley Nichols (*It Happened Tomorrow,* 1944), Lamar Trotti (*Life Begins at Forty,* 1935), Harry Kurnitz (*Shadow of the Thin Man,* 1941, and *They Got Me Covered,* 1943), Dalton Trumbo (*Road Gang,* 1936), Billy Wilder (*Ace in the Hole,* 1951), Dore Schary (*Washington Story,* 1952, and

Lonelyhearts, 1959), Sam Hellman *(Stanley and Livingstone,* 1939), John C. Moffit *(Murder with Pictures,* 1936), Norman Krasna *(Hollywood Speaks,* 1932), James Poe *(The Big Knife,* 1955), William Bowers *(Assignment Paris,* 1952), Lawrence Kimble *(Off the Record,* 1939), and Michael Fessier *(Exclusive Story,* 1936).

Over the years, scores of screen writers who had once been in the news-reporting business were involved, either as writers, co-writers, producers, and/or directors, in hundreds of movies in which reporters or editors were portrayed as either leading or key supporting characters.

Among them, these former newsmen did much to invent (or recall) the language and behavior that became the identifying symbols, and ultimately the cliches, of onscreen newspapermen. These fictional journalists always wore their hats — on the backs of their heads — in the office, nipped frequently at whiskey bottles conveniently stashed in bottom desk drawers; treated pimple-faced copy boys like retarded slaves; cradled telephones between ear and shoulder as they dictated flawless lead paragraphs to unseen rewrite men; told their bosses how the paper should be run; threatened with monotonous regularity to quit this rotten business and take a cushy public

His Girl Friday. For this remake of *The Front Page* (with Rosalind Russell as Hildy and Helen Mack as Molly) director Howards Hawks assembled a fine crew of experienced movie reporters. Seen above are Roscoe Karns, Cliff Edward, and Frank Jenks. (Columbia, 1940)

relations job; looked down their bulbous noses at women who worked at newspapers, sniffed out scandal with the unerring instincts of bird dogs; figured out solutions to criminal conundrums that had baffled invariably inept police; went to the most outlandish lengths to scoop their rivals; and managed to find telephones in the unlikeliest places just in time to call the city desk and bark out that most inevitable of all movie newspaper cliches, "Stop the presses!"

Since screen writing involves more than dialogue, these same ex-reporters (or, at least, some of them) helped develop a literature of appropriate visual cliches as well: the bank of presses rolling, the wire rack sending up completed, folded newspapers, the bundle of tied newspapers being dumped off the truck and landing on the sidewalk, thus enabling us to read the headline ("DA Promises Break in Jones Case in 48 Hours"), the tattered, comic-looking, elderly newsies hawking these late editions, the over-the-shoulder shot of the front page being read by some unseen person, followed by a shot of a pair of hands — belonging, of course, to the gambler, crooked banker, or "syndicate" leader who doesn't want a break in the Jones case — angrily crumpling the newspaper, while an evil voice vows revenge on the "smart" reporter who was pursuing the story.

Hecht and MacArthur, both long since resting comfortably in that Big City Room in the Sky, cannot be blamed for (much less credited with) all of this. But The Front Page, coming when it did and being so engagingly executed — originally directed, incidentally, by yet another onetime newspaperman, George S. Kaufman — could not help but exercise a considerable influence over those Hollywood producers, good, bad, or indifferent, part of whose creed was the aforementioned dogma of Me-Tooism.

Lest it seem that too much emphasis is being laid on the importance of one play or movie, consider the long and healthy history of The Front Page. First produced on Broadway in 1928, it became a successful film in 1931. Nine years later, it was revamped into an equally delightful vehicle for Rosalind Russell (as a female Hildy Johnson) and Cary Grant (as Walter Burns) titled His Girl Friday.

On the Broadway stage it was revived in 1946, with Lew Parker and Arnold Moss in the leading roles, and again in 1968, with Anthony George and Robert Ryan, the latter revival also touring. Of course, there is no way of counting the number of local, professional, semipro, amateur, or school productions of The Front Page that have been staged across the country in the intervening years.

And in 1974, the then forty-six year-old play was filmed a third time, with Jack Lemmon as Hildy and Walter Matthau as Burns.

Not too many American plays of this century have been revived as many times. Fewer still have had so far-reaching an impact on the style and content of so many movies.

2

THE REPORTER AS CRIME BUSTER

The aggressive, enterprising newspaper reporter learns early in his career (if not in journalism school) to "get the story." If he is covering public affairs, he must learn to dig deeper than the handouts of politicians intend him to. If he is dogging a celebrity, he must use whatever ingenuity he can muster to bypass the usual barriers placed in his path. If he is covering a fire or some other spot news story, he must seek out witnesses to get their versions of what took place.

Somewhere along the line, some newsmen have been known, while covering crime stories, to try to out-sleuth the police. No doubt, any large daily paper can delve into its files and find clippings proving one or another of its reporters has succeeded in this area. More often than not, you'll find framed blowups of front pages with evidence of such feats decorating the lobbies of newspaper buildings.

It was probably inevitable, therefore, that screen writers with newspaper backgrounds should dredge up memories of such instances, experienced or witnessed, and use them as bases for newspaper movie scripts. And since Hollywood "plots" have a tendency to multiply about as prolifically as rabbits do, by the mid-1930's movie audiences were up to their craning necks in omniscient reporters who spent about two minutes at their typewriters for every thirty they devoted to outwitting patently retarded police forces.

In fairness to these movie plotters, it should be stated again that successful theatrical drama, in any medium, is an extension of life rather than a reflection of it. Had *The Front Page* been more "accurate," it almost surely would have been less entertaining. Perhaps in the interest of truth, some newspaper films have attempted to place the reporter in his more realistic place: as an observer of the human condition, occasionally commenting on the actions and attitudes around him but not really being a participant. Almost invariably, such films have failed to find large audiences.

Conversely, newspaper films in which the leading men (or women) were up to their unremovable hats in trouble, chasing crooks, beating both the police and their own rivals to the scenes of crimes, and otherwise behaving unbelievably, have met with far more public favor. A hero, after all, must behave like a hero; he can't hold the viewer's attention by sitting around rewriting handouts. Moreover, there was more glamour in the witty newsman who told his editor off, proved the stupidity of the authorities, faced up fearlessly to hoodlums, and occasionally got drunk, than in the nine-to-five humdrum existence the audience went to the movies to forget.

The Front Page also indicated that a proper balance between melodrama and comedy was a winning combination in the newspaper movie. However obvious that example may seem, it was often ignored in the next couple of decades, and the results were usually less satisfying. As a rule, those films that kept a sense of humor, that didn't take themselves too seriously, proved more palatable than those in which the crime-busting became the focal point, rather than the fun.

A good early example was *Hi, Nellie* a 1934 Warner Brothers effort whipped up by ex-journalist Roy Chanslor, which proved successful enough to spawn at least one official remake and numerous imitations.

Hi, Nellie. Paul Muni was the managing editor who was demoted to the advice-to-the-lovelorn column. (Warner Brothers, 1934)

The Nellie of *Hi, Nellie* was Paul Muni, an acknowledged star after *Scarface* and *I Am a Fugitive from a Chain Gang*. His leading lady was Glenda Farrell, who was destined to put in considerable time in movie newsrooms over the next decade. At the opening of this bright film, Miss Farrell was the Nellie of the title — that is, the otherwise anonymous writer of the paper's daily "Advice to the Lovelorn" column — and Muni was to blame. She, it seems, had flopped on a big story and Muni, the tyrannical managing editor, chose this traditional punishment for her. (One can't help wondering if the likes of Abigail Van Buren and Ann Landers are amused by the Hollywood notion that this branch of journalism, which made them rich, was so consistently treated as a punishment for errant reporters.)

But fate has a way of catching up with characters in movies and by the second reel Muni has likewise blown a big story, and when the publisher (Berton Churchill) can't break Muni's contract he resorts to demoting his managing editor to writing the "Nellie" column. Cruel colleagues make his next few entrances hell by greeting him with, "Hi, Nellie!" Thus humiliated, Muni upholds another journalistic tradition by turning to booze to soothe his bruised ego, and it is glorious Glenda who gives him a talking to and straightens him out. Pulling himself together, Muni turns the "Nellie" column into the hit of the paper, and Fate rewards him by allowing him to stumble over a clue that not only revives the story that had been his undoing, but gives him a new angle that helps him ultimately to prove that he was right all along and everyone else — police, publisher, the world — was wrong. (Who but a former newspaperman could concoct such a gratifying daydream!)

However unlikely that plot sounds now, it worked then. In addition, the movie had a lively battle-of-the-sexes relationship between Muni and Miss Farrell. Muni then and later generally regarded as a "serious" actor, still managed to hoke it up engagingly, getting more than adequate mileage out of lines like: "You tell His Honor I'll rip him apart on Page One tomorrow."

From the earliest days, Hollywood producers have periodically displayed a strange knack for making unfathomable casting decisions. A famous 1964 example was Warner Brothers' casting of Audrey Hepburn in *My Fair Lady* after Julie Andrews had captivated theatergoers as the stage's Liza Doolittle.

(A more bizarre example was the 1942 movie, *Syncopation*, a sort of sketchy history of jazz whose cast of characters included a black trumpeter. In a burst of logic, the producers picked Rex Stewart, then a featured trumpeter with Duke Ellington's orchestra, to play the role. He was coached in acting, and turned in a reasonably creditable performance. But somewhere along the way, the producers decided they didn't like his trumpet playing, so the horn of Bunny Berigan was dubbed in.)

But as early as 1931, a Hollywood producer—Howard Hughes, no less—made one of those mystifying choices. As mentioned earlier, Lee Tracy had been a smash hit as Hildy Johnson in the 1928 stage version of *The Front Page.* He had, in fact, made several movies in the intervening years, thus, one would think, enhancing his value as a "name." Yet, for reasons long since lost track of, Tracy did not play Hildy on the screen.

Nevertheless, a year after *The Front Page* was filmed, Tracy played the first of several newspaper roles in films and in the next few years became virtually the personification of the smart-aleck newspaperman.

In that year, 1932, he played two movie newspapermen. The first was in *The Strange Love of Molly Louvain,* in which he was a nice reporter trying to help Ann Dvorak, a lady with a past. A few months later, in *Blessed Event,* he was a glib, unscrupulous columnist who, nevertheless, was brave enough to stand up to the thugs who crossed his righteous path.

The following year, Tracy starred in *Advice to the Lovelorn,* which might sound as if it were swiped from *Hi, Nellie,* but in fact descended from a greater height. According to

the credits, it was "inspired by" the then-new Nathanael West story, "Miss Lonelyhearts." Unhappily it was inspired by nothing more elevating than a wish to make money and actually bore little resemblance to either the West story or the Paul Muni film, which wasn't released until 1934. In *Advice to the Lovelorn,* Tracy played a newsman who got drunk and was punished by being demoted to the advice column. But the story soon slipped into routine crime melodrama, brightened chiefly by Tracy's breezy style.

Tracy's career as a movie reporter stretched on — dropping into categories that will be dealt with in other chapters — for several more years. In 1937, for instance, he was back to playing demon newshound, tracking down bad guys in *Behind the Headlines.* By the 1940's there were so many movie reporters helping to blur what was left of the old Hecht-MacArthur image that Lee Tracy was in for quite a few rather lean years. But he had a satisfying comeback in 1960, playing a wily old president in Gore Vidal's political comedy-drama, *The Best Man.* Once again, after a quarter of a century, Tracy's nasal voice and iconoclastic manner made him the toast of Broadway. This time, happily, when the movie version was made, Tracy repeated his stage role and won new critical plaudits.

And what of the man who had been given Tracy's role in the movie version of *The Front Page*? That was Pat O'Brien, then a newcomer to Hollywood, launching a movie career that would span four decades. During that time he was to play Irish cops, slum priests, smooth-talking hucksters, Cagney rivals, and, of course, an assortment of newspapermen. O'Brien's appealing style, his flair for rapid-fire talk, and his worldy, slightly bored look, all combined to make him a durable favorite with movie fans.

He was an immediate hit, and in the year following *The Front Page,* he continued to play newspapermen. In *Hollywood Speaks* (1932), he was a glib movieland reporter who went out on a limb to help Genevieve Tobin get a screen test. In *The Final Edition,* the same year, O'Brien was the tough editor who had to go out and rescue reporter Mae Clarke when she got trapped by the killer she was tracking down.

Blessed Event. Isobel Jewel, Lee Tracy, and Mary Brian were the principals in this newspaper yarn. (Warner Brothers, 1932)

Advice to the Lovelorn. Lee Tracy was the adviser and
Sterling Holloway his impressionable friend. (United
Artists, 1933)

Behind the Headlines. Few newspaper films could
avoid a scene in a bar. This one had Diane Gibson and
Lee Tracy. (RKO, 1937)

Back in Circulation. Pat O'Brien and Ben Welden are in disagreement, which may account for the gun in Pat's hand. (Warner Brothers, 1937)

In 1933, O'Brien was an ace reporter in *The World Gone Mad,* ferreting out a crooked banker. For a few years, he broke away from newspaper movies, playing instead second leads to Dick Powell, James Cagney, and Henry Fonda. But by 1937 he returned to the city room in *Back in Circulation*, this time as an editor making life rough but romantic for reporter Joan Blondell. Two years later, they did it all over again in *Off the Record*. And eighteen years after that, in 1957, O'Brien starred in *Kill Me Tomorrow*, made in England, in which he played a crime reporter who needs money to finance his ailing son's imminent operation. With typical enterprise, he brings to justice a ring of criminals and thus averts insolvency.

Although Lee Tracy and Pat O'Brien were "pioneers" in projecting the screen image of the newspaperman, they had no monopoly in the field. From the early 1930's on, many of Hollywood's top stars have played newspapermen, including Clark Gable, Cary Grant, Fred MacMurray, James Cagney, Humphrey Bogart, James Stewart, Tyrone Power, Edward G. Robinson, and the still-revered Spencer Tracy.

In the space of a dozen years, for example, Spencer Tracy played six newspaper roles, with varying degrees of box-office success. During his lengthy career, Clark Gable played newspapermen in nine movies. Stewart has played half a dozen newsmen, as has Cary Grant. Cagney, Robinson, and MacMurray four each, William Holden, Gregory Peck and Humphrey Bogart two or three each.

With very few exceptions, all these films were made when the actors mentioned were stars. They were A pictures, made mostly by the bigger studios, with reputable directors and writers involved, with well-known leading ladies and solid supporting casts. Whether or not they were all smash hits, they must still be regarded as major movies dealing with newspaper toilers in one category or another.

But over the years — and especially during the 1930s and 1940s — for every A newspaper movie there were probably half a dozen B pictures dealing with newsmen. These tended to vary from acceptable to poor to downright awful, and the worst of them no doubt had a certain amount to do with the decline of both newspaper movies and B pictures.

Nevertheless, such films deserve to be included in this gallery if only because they had as much influence on the public's consciousness of the American press, however distorted or romanticized, as the bigger A films. Some of them were B pictures, in terms of quality, even before that pejorative term was coined.

In 1932, Ricardo Cortez, then a popular star, played the lead in *Is My Face Red?*, which also featured Helen Twelvetrees and Robert Armstrong, the latter as a rival newsman. Cortez was one of those Lee Tracy-type vain, unethical columnists, disliked for his ego, resented for his success. He announces a murder in his column before the police give out the story and pretty soon he's in deep trouble — all of it dissolving into air by the final fadeout.

The following year, James Cagney made a partial switch from criminal to newsman. In *Picture Snatcher* (1933), he played an ex-con working for a tabloid and charged with taking sneaky pictures. At one point, he sneaks his camera into an execution and photographs the grisly event, thus causing great embarrassment to his girlfriend's father, a police officer. But Cagney later squares everything by managing to photograph a murderer in action, thereby helping to convict the killer. Opposite Cagney in this effort was Alice White, and

Is My Face Red? Ricardo Cortez was the blushing newsman, Helen Twelvetrees his concerned lady. (RKO, 1932)

Ralph Bellamy was seen as a tippling newsman.

Also in 1933, Ben Lyon was a daring reporter going after some smugglers in *I Cover the Waterfront*. Lyon's love was Claudette Colbert, whose father (Ernest Torrence) was smuggling aliens into San Diego, sewn, if you please, into the bellies of huge dead sharks. But, as usual, a reporter's blood runs thicker than love, so he exposed the smuggling racket. And Claudette forgave him.

George Brent and Bette Davis, then two of Warners most popular stars, got into the newspaper business in 1935 with *Front Page Woman*. They were rival reporters in this sex-battle comedy-melodrama, he insisting that "women make rotten newspapermen," she determined to prove him wrong. The film involved all manner of mayhem, double-crossing, impossible editors ranting at the ineptness of their underlings, and so on. At one point, Brent eavesdrops on a jury, gets advance word of the verdict, and then phones his paper: "Hold the four-star for a stop-press!" To further infuriate Bette, he also planted phoney "not guilty" slips for her to find, thus leading her to call her paper with the wrong story.

One of the ludicrous devices, in this and too many other newspaper films, was having the star reporter dictate his story — often right from the press room, with his rivals supposedly turning suddenly deaf — so that we, the audience, could hear its deathless prose. Dramatically, that was more effective than watching somebody type his story and then having an

The Picture Snatcher. James Cagney had one of the less
glamorous jobs, but Alice White didn't seem to mind.
(Warner Brothers, 1933)

I Cover the Waterfront. That was Ben Lyon's beat in this one, and Claudette Colbert was his girl. (United Artists, 1933)

Front Page Woman. Newsman George Brent and his trusty aid, Roscoe Karns, are up to no good in this scene. (Warner Brothers, 1935)

over-the-shoulder shot enabling us to read what he'd written. But now that these vintage films are seen mostly on television, it would be impossible to read their stories in the typewriters, anyhow.

Like any other year, 1936 had its share of newspaper yarns, including *The Girl on the Front Page,* a comedy in which Edmund Lowe was the managing editor of a newspaper inherited by Gloria Stuart; and *Adventure in Manhattan,* in which Joel McCrea was the crime-solving reporter and Jean Arthur played the actress he falls in love with.

One film that was regarded as a cut above the average (but seems woefully dated now) was *Exclusive,* made in 1937 by Paramount, with no less than three former newspapermen

The Girl on the Front Page. Edmund Lowe was the editor, Gloria Stuart the heiress who owned the paper. (Universal, 1936)

Adventure in Manhattan. Newsman Joel McCrea faces up to Reginald Owen in this news-crime melodrama. (Columbia, 1936)

Exclusive. Fred MacMurray and Charlie Ruggles were both pals and newsmen in this lively film. (Paramount, 1937)

film had some lively dialogue — mostly in defense of respectable journalism — and at least one memorable comedy scene in which Fred and Charles, after consuming all the beer in a refrigerator, try to find out if that little light really goes out when you close the door. (Unhappily, this scene has sometimes been edited out of the film on television.) In another scene when MacMurray and Ruggles get drunk and are delivered home in a police ambulance, an outraged neighbor observes: ''Newspaper people! A disgrace to the street.''

By the mid-1930s, B pictures about newspapermen, disgraceful or otherwise, were coming from all directions. Actors like Kent Taylor, Michael Whalen, Jack Oakie, Preston Foster, Wallace Ford, Brian Donlevy, William Gargan, Lynne Overman, James Dunn, Lew Ayres, Donald Woods, Roger Pryor, Stuart Erwin, Warren Hull, and others played crime reporters, feet on desks, hats pushed back, abusing their editors, pushing their way

taking a hand in the script, and starring Fred MacMurray.

In the story, MacMurray and Charlie Ruggles were fellow reporters on a ''respectable'' newspaper. Racketeer Lloyd Nolan bought a rival paper and turned it into a scandal sheet, primarily to smear and otherwise attack his enemies.

Frances Farmer, as Ruggles's daughter and Fred's girl friend, takes a job as a reporter on Nolan's rag and proceeds to gum up the works—causing a disgraced politician to commit suicide, bringing on a libel suit when she charges that the elevators in a department store are unsafe. To avoid the suit, Nolan is not above fixing the elevators, thus causing a dreadful accident. By the time Frances comes to her senses, her father has been killed by Nolan's hoods, the townspeople have mobbed the scandal sheet, and MacMurray has been in and out of a hospital.

Despite the extreme melodramatics, the

Regis Toomey. Among other roles, this veteran actor appeared many times as a reporter.

Double feature. Two regular reporters were Stuart Erwin, (center), and Wallace Ford (right).

A Man Betrayed. Editor Joseph Crehan (seated) and reporter Wallace Ford played many press parts. In the center is Edward Ellis. (Republic, 1941)

Star Reporter. Warren Hull (left center) was the title character in this B picture. (Monogram, 1939)

The Midnight Patrol. Reporter Regis Toomey apparently hasn't pleased his frowning boss. (Monogram, 1932)

through police lines, solving perplexing crimes, downing drinks, calling in scoops, and generally being some strangely acceptable mixture of obnoxious and winning.

The names of characters — particularly secondary ones — also settled into nice, recognizable ruts. We were deluged with guys named Scoop and Flash and Ace. When Chick Chandler played a photographer in *While New York Sleeps* (1938) he was named Snapper. Similarly, when Glenda Farrell portrayed a photographer in *Exposed,* the same year, the character was called Click. And Roscoe Karns, who played so many second-lead reporters and photographers that he really should have been retired on a pension from the American Newspaper Guild, was forever get-

Roscoe Karns. No self-respecting movie newspaper could have managed without him on the staff, often as a photographer.

The Daring Young Man. Mae Clarke and James Dunn were both after the same story, a prison exposé. (20th Century-Fox, 1935)

ting stuck with characters named Toots and Mopsy and Happy.

But, never mind. The B pictures about newspaper people droned on through the years, each one adding a little cliche to the mangled image of journalism, each offering some combination of crime and detection, male-female rivalry, plus increasingly stale city-room wisecracks and enervating shots of rolling presses and wildly spinning front pages that hurtled toward the audience, stopping upright so the unremarkable headline could be read.

In 1935, James Dunn and Mae Clarke were rival reporters in *The Daring Young Man,* both assigned to cover prison conditions. Dunn uncovers a criminal (Warren Hymer) who is hiding out — in jail, mind you — after robbing the United States Treasury. The same year, James Dunn played a sports columnist deeply in debt to some sinister gamblers in *The Pay-Off.*

In 1936, William Gargan, another perennial B picture newsman, made *Man Hunt,* one of several unrelated films with that same title. In this one, Gargan was a reporter hot on the trail of gangster Ricardo Cortez. (Incidentally, the Gargans had a pretty good foothold in newspaper movies in those days. While William was playing reporters, brother Edward was seen as one of those dumb cops that reporters so often encountered. They never appeared together in those respective roles, but between them they made a dozen newspaper films.)

In *Human Cargo* (1936), Brian Donlevy and

The Pay-Off. Patricia Ellis was James Dunn's leading lady this time. He played a sports columnist. (Warner Brothers, 1935)

35

Human Cargo. Reporter Brian Donlevy is on to a big story here, and you can be sure he got it, too. (20th Century-Fox, 1936)

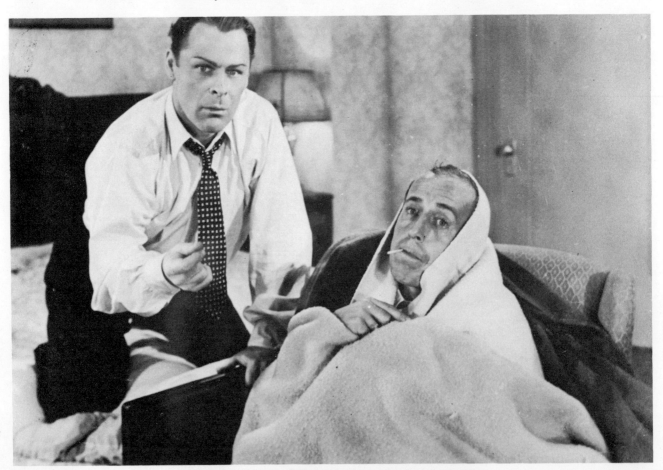

Half Angel. That's Charlie Butterworth under the blanket, and newsman Brian Donlevy trying to unscramble the plot. (20th Century-Fox, 1936)

Claire Trevor were competing newshounds, but it was Donlevy who managed to get the goods on a smuggling ring, unaided by the authorities. And the same year, in *Half Angel*, Donlevy was a reporter who, single-handed, cleared Frances Dee of a false charge of murder.

Jack Oakie, the jovial *boule de suif* who usually confined his antics to musical comedies set on college campuses, turned reporter in a pleasant lark titled *Florida Special* (1936), in which he got involved with some jewel thieves aboard a train.

The same year, George Murphy, sans tap shoes, turned reporter in *Woman Trap*, with Gertrude Michael and Sidney Blackmer.

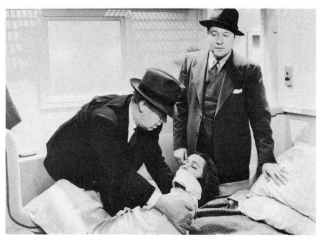

Florida Special. J. Farrell MacDonald and reporter Jack Oakie are the rescuers, Frances Drake the girl. (Paramount, 1936)

Woman Trap. Reporter George Murphy and Sidney Blackmer barely kept apart by Gertrude Michael. (Paramount, 1936)

(Roscoe Karns played Mopsy, the photographer.) Once again, the reporter deserted his typewriter to go after a gang of jewel thieves.

And also in 1936, Roger Pryor was a fearless journalist in *Missing Girls,* in which he was sent to prison for contempt of court. While there, he unearthed a plot to assassinate a senator, which gave him a scoop and the G-men a defendent. Pryor had earlier played newspapermen in *The Headline Woman* and *One Thousand Dollars a Minute*, both in 1935.

There Goes My Girl. Gene Raymond, in evening clothes, was the reporter and Joseph Crehan the editor. (RKO, 1937)

The Headline Woman. Roger Pryor, a busy B-picture reporter, was the star of this one. (Monogram, 1935)

The following year, 1937, Gene Raymond and Ann Sothern, who had already appeared together in a couple of light comedies, did the newspaper office version of man-vs.-woman in *There Goes My Girl.*

Michael Whalen, another B picture regular in the 1930s was a reporter in *Time Out for Murder* (1937), solving a murder and saving an innocent man. His sidekick was Chick Chandler, the second-string Roscoe Karns, playing photographer "Snapper" Doolan. The following year, Whalen and Chandler did it all over again—beating the police and the opposition papers—in *While New York Sleeps* (1938).

When it wasn't Pryor or Donlevy or Whalen, it was Kent Taylor. In 1938, Taylor was a dauntless managing editor in *A Girl with Ideas*. The girl was Wendy Barrie, and her ideas had to do with running the paper she had just inherited—the one managed by Taylor.

The compulsion to make more and more newspaper films went unchecked throughout the decade and, in time, both the titles and the themes showed signs of strain. There was Lew Ayres in *Murder with Pictures (1936)* and *King of the Newsboys* (1938). There was Norman Foster in *Behind the Evidence* (1935), as a society reporter who solved crimes virtually between editions. (When a rewrite man took his story over the phone, the rest of the staff crowded around to listen, implying this was a one-story newspaper.) There was *Jailbreak* (1936), in which reporter Craig Reynolds solved a murder while in jail. There was *We're Only Human* (1936), with Jane Wyatt as a bright eyed reporter and Preston Foster as a tough but honest cop.

But the real signs of desperation came with the use of ever-younger players in newspaper yarns: Jackie Cooper in *Newsboys' Home* (1938), Bonita Granville in *Nancy Drew, Reporter* (1939), and Jimmy Lydon in *Henry Aldrich, Editor* (1942). Even before that, Lew Ayres had been in *King of the Newsboys* (1938) with a whole platoon of male moppets, and back in 1936, even little Jane Withers had sat down at a typewriter in *Gentle Julia*, in which Tom Brown played a young reporter pal of Jane's.

Wayne Morris, who came along in the late 1930s (gaining fame as Kid Gallahad), turned

Time Out for Murder. Gloria Stuart, Chick Chandler,
and Michael Whalen, journalists all. (20th Century-
Fox, 1938)

A Girl with Ideas. Only in the movies would a managing
editor sit on the copy desk. This one is Kent Taylor.
(Universal, 1938)

Newsboys' Home. Jackie Cooper may have been sent to the home for dropping all those papers. (Universal, 1939)

Henry Aldrich, Editor. Never mind the pen being mightier than the sword. In a pinch, a wooden plank will do. That's Jimmy Lydon, as Henry Aldrich, about to whomp his cringing adversary. (Paramount, 1942)

Gentle Julia. They laughed when she sat down at the typewriter. No wonder: it was Jane Withers. (20th Century-Fox, 1936)

Double Alibi. Wayne Morris and Margaret Lindsay were the stars, but they couldn't have gotten through it without Roscoe Karns and his camera. (Universal, 1940)

up as a reporter in 1940 in *Double Alibi,* with Margaret Lindsay as his leading lady and the ubiquitous Roscoe Karns with his trusty camera. And nine years later, Morris was a brash reporter again, this time with Janis Paige to help him solve the murder, in *The House across the Street.*

By the early 1940s the brash, irreverent, somewhat offensive reporter was a long-familiar yet still acceptable movie type. If any one B picture of the era managed to combine all the clichés of the genre, it was probably *Nine Lives Are Not Enough* (1941), starring Ronald Reagan as a boastful reporter-photographer. ("On the strength of my story and my story alone, he's behind bars," he brags to his colleagues in an early scene.)

This movie had everything. The dumb cop

The House across the Street. Wayne Morris and Janis Paige seem puzzled, but they solved the crime. (Warner Brothers, 1949)

Nine Lives Are Not Enough. Ronald Reagan, future governor, was a reporter-photographer in this one. (Warner Brothers, 1941)

and planning to assign him to — what else? — the advice-to-the-lovelorn column. But, wait. There's still another switcheroo. Socialite Joan buys the paper and appoints Reagan managing editor. (Imagine, if they hadn't run out of film, Joseph Crehan might have ended up writing the advice column.)

That tired advice-to-the-lovelorn gimmick turned up yet again the following year in a Warners movie titled *You Can't Escape Forever.* (It's a toss-up whether Warner Brothers or Columbia holds the record for regurgitating and then recycling previously used story material.) This one had George Brent and Brenda Marshall in the leading roles, and was simply a remake of the old standby, *Hi, Nellie,* with Brent this time being demoted to the advice column, only to rise again triumphant, with a scoop in one hand and Brenda in the other.

The 1940s gave us a mixture of old and new reporters. William Gargan, a veteran film newsman from the previous decade, was still

was played by Ed Brophy, a past master at conveying stupidity, his superior was James Gleason, another expert at playing it dumb. The managing editor was Joseph Crehan, as familiar a figure in movie newspaper offices as was Roscoe Karns behind a camera.

Reagan, hot on the trail of a murder yarn, is not above removing distributor caps from the cars of rival reporters and even policemen to allow him to keep ahead of everyone else. When he gets fired from his job for inaccurate reporting, Reagan doggedly stays on the story, driven now, in addition, by his attraction to Joan Perry, a socialite in distress.

As if familiar with Hollywood tradition, dumb cops Brophy and Gleason fall into the pattern of taking their orders from Reagan — by now an unemployed reporter — on what strategy they should pursue to solve the crime.

And, to top off this tower of triteness, the movie's "classic" ending has the city editor (Howard De Silva) double-crossing Reagan

You Can't Escape Forever. George Brent and Brenda Marhsall starred in this remake of *Hi, Nellie.* (Warner Brothers, 1941)

Midnight Manhunt. Even a crap game can be interrupted for a news break, as in this film. That's reporter William Gargan on the phone. (Paramount, 1945)

at it. In 1945, he was a determined, anything-for-a-scoop reporter in *Midnight Manhunt*.

Lloyd Nolan, another established player (mostly, but not exclusively, in B pictures) had another good role as a cynical reporter in *Behind the News* (1941), with Robert Armstrong in the supporting cast. Armstrong, along with Regis Toomey, Wallace Ford, Eddie Quillan, and Dick Purcell, played many supporting roles as reporters.

Tom Neal, who made a number of minor films in the 1930s, starred in *Crime, Inc.* (1945), as a reporter facing a prison term for refusing to divulge information. But he eventually rounded up an assortment of heavies that included Lionel Atwill and Leo Carrillo.

Behind the News. Lloyd Nolan was the newsman this time, and Doris Davenport the troubled-looking girl. (Republic, 1941)

Eddie Quillan. Usually in B pictures, frequently as a brash young newsman.

Lee Bowman, who made a living mostly by playing playboys in evening clothes, was a columnist in *The Walls Came Tumbling Down* (1945), investigating the death of a priest.

Dane Clark, a newcomer to films in the 1940s, was a sleuthing Broadway columnist in *Her Kind of Man* (1946), with Janis Paige as the "her" and Zachary Scott as the bad guy.

In 1947, veteran George Brent was back at the newspaper game, teamed with Joan Blondell in *The Corpse Came C.O.D.* Both were reporters trying to clear up some Hollywood murders.

Dennis O'Keefe, another in the line of blarney-blessed Irishmen, was a reporter in *Abandoned* (1949), digging up the dope on a baby-adoption racket.

And Alan Ladd, who had shot to stardom as a tough guy in the mid-1940s (after some years in small parts), was a tough reporter in *Chicago Deadline* (1949), brooding over some involved skullduggery but eventually tracking down the underworld types responsible.

As the 1940s gave way to the 1950s, the

Crime, Inc. Reporter Tom Neal and his lady friend are threatened by syndicate heavies Lionel Atwill and Leo Carillo. (Prodecess Releasing Corp., 1945)

The Walls Came Tumbling Down. Lee Bowman, center,
was a columnist here. With him are Edgar Buchanan
and Marguerite Chapman. (Columbia, 1945)

The Corpse Came C.O.D. George Brent and Joan
Blondell, two veteran film journalists, starred in this
one. In the middle is Jim Bannon. (Columbia, 1947)

Abandoned. Newshawk Dennis O'Keefe was on the
trail of child abductors. At right is Charles Jordan.
(Universal-International, 1949)

Chicago Deadline. Tough guy Alan Ladd turned reporter this time. With him is June Havoc. (Paramount,
1949)

Bannerline. Editor Warner Anderson looks over Keefe
Brasselle's copy. (MGM, 1951)

crime-solving reporter was becoming a pretty tiresome figure, but the was still kept alive, especially in B pictures.

In 1951, there was Keefe Brasselle in *Bannerline,* playing an honest young reporter bent on exposing corruption and such in his town. Also in 1951, Robert Hutton was a reporter in *The Racket,* which had Robert Mitchum as a cop and Robert Ryan as a racketeer.

Other journalistic B movies of the time included *Hot News* (1953), with Stanley Clements and Gloria Henry, *The Big Tip-Off* (1955), with Richard Conte poking into a charity-fund racket and tripping over a murder, and Dana Andrews in *While the City Sleeps* (1956), as a crime-probing newsman.

Again emphasizing the use of key words in newspaper movie titles in those days, there was *Headline Hunters* (1955), with Rod Cameron and Julie Bishop. Back in 1937, Frankie Darro, a pint-sized favorite in serials and B pictures, had made *Headline Crasher,* and there had already been *Headline Shooters and Headline Woman.*

Thus far, most of the movies mentioned have involved crime-busting reporters as the leading characters in the stories. There have, of course, been many other films in which reporters were involved as secondary or supporting characters, and it might be well to sprinkle in a few examples.

To begin with, there was *Shadow of the Thin Man* (1941), the second in that enormously successful series about Nick and Nora Charles (William Powell and Myrna Loy), Hollywood's most appealing amateur sleuths. There were two newspapermen prominent in

The Racket. Newsman Robert Hutton comes to Lisabeth Scott's help. The officer is Walter Sande. (RKO, 1951)

Hot News. Stanley Clements offers a watch to Gloria Henry. For a small-budget film, he must have been a highly paid reporter. (Allied Artists, 1953)

The Big Tip-Off. No newspaper's day could be complete without finding at least one body. The reporter here is Richard Conte. (Allied Artists, 1955)

While the City Sleeps. Even love-making has to wait while reporter Dana Andrews phones in a story. (RKO, 1956)

Headline Hunters. The seasoned reporter here was Rod Cameron, (left.) With him are Julie Bishop and Ben Cooper. (Republic, 1955)

Headline Shooters. William Gargan and Frances Dee went after the same story in this yarn about newsreel reporters. (RKO, 1933)

Personal Secretary. Newsman William Gargan again, this time with Andy Devine as his sidekick. (Universal, 1938)

the cast (and plot) of this movie. One was Barry Nelson, the other Alan Baxter. While Powell was up to his charming quips in solving a racetrack murder, reporter Nelson tried to help him and found himself charged with killing Baxter. Of course, Powell cleared up the whole mess.

In 1942, Lynne Overman had a good supporting role as a reporter in *Roxie Hart,* which starred Ginger Rogers and Adolphe Menjou. It was a clever comedy and Overman's skill as an actor was a marked asset to it.

In a more serious film of 1947, *Boomerang,* Dana Andrews headed the cast as a stubborn prosecuting attorney who keeps sensing flaws in the state's case against an accused mur-

Shadow of the Thin Man. William Powell and Myrna Loy flank two supporters, Henry O'Neill and Barry Nelson, the latter playing a reporter. (MGM, 1941)

Lynne Overman. This dryly amusing actor played his share of newspaper roles.

Boomerang. Sam Levene was a convincing newsman in this drama. With him is Taylor Holmes. (20th Century-Fox, 1947)

derer. Somewhat in the background, but contributing a fine performance to this altogether admirable Elia Kazan film, was Sam Levene, as a no-nonsense newspaperman helping Andrews to track down the truth.

And in 1956, there was *Ransom,* in which Glenn Ford was the father of a kidnapped child. He is stubborn and bold enough (if not plain reckless) to risk the child's life by refusing to pay the demanded ransom. Leslie Nielsen played the hard-nosed newspaperman who encouraged Ford in this dangerous experiment.

As can be seen from some of the newspaper films of the 1950s, the crime-busting reporter had pretty well worn out his welcome. Some attempts were made to keep him going by having him delve into more unusual crimes — phony charity funds, baby adoption rackets, etc—but it was becoming clear that the old-fashioned, hat-on-the-back-of-the-head, wise-cracking reporter was no longer a hero that movie audiences could take too seriously.

Perhaps his last desperate gasp was signaled in 1953 when Donald O'Connor and his talking mule turned reporter-sleuths in one of the more lamentable movies in that generally undistinguished series. It was called *Francis Covers the Big Town,* and it covered nobody concerned with anything remotely resembling glory.

In its first scene, O'Connor and mule arrive in New York, broke, and O'Connor muses: ''Let's see, what would I be good at?...I think the newspaper business.''

In the next scene, he's working as a copy boy and doling out scoop-making bits of information to seasoned reporters, inside stuff presumably gathered by the talking, and understandably big-eared, mule. Contrary to the

Ransom. The man pounding the desk is Leslie Nielsen, a reporter who opposed paying ransom. Seated is Glenn Ford, father of a kidnapped child. (MGM, 1956)

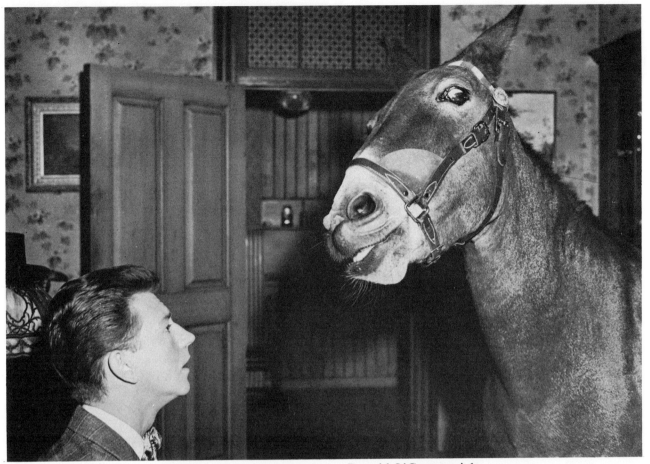

Francis Covers the Big Town. Donald O'Connor picks up the latest dope from his gabby mule. (Universal, 1953)

Name the Woman. Like most movie reporters, Richard Cromwell spent half his time on the telephone. (Columbia, 1934)

old saw, every picture is NOT worth a thousand words, and this was one of those.

The George Brents and William Gargans and Kent Taylors and Pat O'Briens and all those other glib, amateur sleuths of the city room had had their days — more than twenty years of them.

But even if the crime-busting reporter was running out of wind, the newspaper film certainly was not. It had, by then, spread out in various different directions, some of which were to prove profitable to the studios and enjoyable to audiences for some years yet.

Mystery Man. The man with the gun (probably the murder weapon) is newsman Robert Armstrong. (Monogram, 1935)

3

THE REPORTER AS SCANDALMONGER

Naive or simplistic as many of them may seem today, movie titles of thirty and forty years ago had, at least, the virtue of clarity. Titles were used not merely to capture attention but also to convey some indication of what the movie might be about.

Movie titles like *Test Pilot* or *Men with Wings* were self-explanatory, as were *Bureau of Missing Persons, The Farmer Takes a Wife,* or *King of the Underworld,* or, for that matter, *Jezebel.*

Compare those to such relatively recent titles as *Thunderbolt and Lightfoot, The Parallax View, The Eiger Sanction,* or even *Five Easy Pieces.* The search for "different" titles can sometimes result in the depressing revelation that nobody cared who or what *T.R. Baskin* was, and may have helped dull *Zabriskie Point.* In the 1930s no producer in his right mind would have agreed to so self-consciously gimmicky a title as *Can Hieronymus Merkin Ever Forget Mercy Humppe and Find True Happiness.*

The advantage of clarity was certainly recognized by those who made newspaper movies in the first two decades of talking pictures. *The Front Page* was a crystal-clear title, as were such subsequent ones as *Front Page Woman, Exclusive, The Final Edition, and Power of the Press.*

People who went to movies in those days had plenty to choose from—several hundred feature films a year from Hollywood, as compared to a fraction of that today—and they indicated early their acceptance of newspaper yarns.

So we had a flood of give-away titles that capitalized on the public's interest in newspapers and their personnel: *Five Star Final, Hot News, Headline Woman, News Is Made at Night, Behind the News, Exclusive Story, The Star Reporter, Off the Record, Big News,* and so on.

But if words like *news* and *headline* and *exclusive* were useful, one word above all others seemed absolutely irresistible: *Scandal.* Gossip has always been a marketable commodity, and any movie title that hinted of it could usually depend on some box-office reaction.

In the first quarter century of sound movies, we had such titles as *Scandal for Sale, Night Club Scandal, Design for Scandal,* plus three different movies titled *Scandal Sheet* and one titled, somewhat misleadingly, *Scandal Street.* In addition there were such tip-off titles as *Libeled Lady, Sued for Libel, Exposed, Over-Exposed, Slander, Scandal, Inc.* and *Secret File Hollywood.* The movies may not always have lived up to the promise of their titles, but by then the tickets had been purchased.

The movie newspaperman who dealt in scandal was another invention of screen writers (usually with a newspaper background) based only loosely on fact. The 1930s were the decade of widely syndicated gossip and name-dropping columnists like Walter Winchell and Ed Sullivan. From Hollywood, you could learn about the personal peccadilloes of the stars from Louella Parsons, Hedda Hopper, or Jimmy Fidler.

Occasionally, some of these "name" journalists delved into matters beyond personal gossip. Winchell, for instance, sometimes used informers to "help" the police locate hoods, and later showed a zealous interest in unearthing "subversive" persons. But for the most part, the real scandalmongers were content to report (with varying degrees of accuracy) the divorces, liaisons, arrivals, departures, parties, elopements, and "madcap" carryings on of theatrical and/or social celebrities.

Understandably, the movie version of the scandal monger went further. He buddied up to runaway heiresses, frequently libeled innocent people, got his paper sued, circled the globe to find missing prominent people, invented phony celebrities to help build circulation, perpetrated all sorts of hoaxes, infiltrated everything from underworld gangs to cafe society to get the "inside" story, and occasionally slipped over into the crime-busting or amateur-sleuth category.

Callousness and cynicism were standard traits of the movie scandalmonger. He was an extension of the Hecht-MacArthur characters in *The Front Page,* combined with the yellow journalists of *Five Star Final.* But, of course, there were to be further variations.

In 1932, Douglas Fairbanks, Jr., was the irreverent gossip columnist in *Love is a Rac-*

The Crusader. Glaring at each other are scandalmonger Ned Sparks and crusading attorney H.B. Warner. (Majestic, 1932)

ket (which also had Lee Tracy as another newsman), hopelessly romanticized in this case. When his glamorous actress girlfriend (Ann Dvorak) jilts him, he rises above his emotions and writes the "scoop."

The *Crusader,* the same year, had H. B. Warner as a crusading district attorney and Ned Sparks as a sour scandal-hunting columnist bent on "exposing" the D.A.'s wife's shady background. ("Reporters, it should be noted," whined one critic, "do not customarily telephone the headlines on their stories, denounce the city administration in their reports, order their first editions held up three hours, or slander the District Attorney and Chief of Police to their several faces." He might as well have saved his breath.)

Also in 1932, Lew Ayres played a gossip columnist in *Okay, America,* picking up tips from all kinds of questionable sources. Ayres, despite his boyish, clean-cut appearance, was rude and arrogant, but clever enough to outwit some gangsters who had kidnapped the daughter of a Washington bigwig. But in the end, he died heroically, gunned down by the mobsters.

Pat O'Brien also lost his life in *Scandal for Sale* (1932), in which he was a reporter sent on a risky transocean flight by a circulation-hungry editor. This editor (Charles Bickford) had an extra reason for exploiting O'Brien: the reporter was sweet on the editor's wife.

Love Is a Racket. Lee Tracy, Ann Dvorak, Douglas Fairbanks, Jr., and Warren Hymer. Notice the newspaper sticking out of Doug's pocket, a standard prop. (Warner Brothers, 1932)

Okay, America. Lew Ayres (seated) was the gossip columnist. At right is Berton Churchill, often a publisher. (Universal, 1932)

Scandal for Sale. Reporter Pat O'Brien flashes his press pass for the skeptical policeman. (Universal, 1932)

Love and Hisses. Ben Bernie and Simone Simon stand behind famous columnist Walter Winchell. (20th Century-Fox, 1938)

Night Club Scandal. Reporter Lynne Overman, with Louise Campbell and Harvey Stephens. (Paramount, 1937)

Exposed. Glenda Farrell was a photographer in this one. At right is Richard Lane. (Universal, 1938)

The movie studios did a bit of exploiting of their own in those days. Walter Winchell made his screen debut, playing himself, in 1937 in *Wake Up and Live,* and appeared again a year later in *Love and Hisses.* Both films were designed to take advantage of the well-publicized "feud" between Winchell and bandleader Ben Bernie, who also appeared in the movies named.*

A more legitimate scandal movie was *Night Club Scandal* (1937), which had Lynne Overman, of the rubbery face and restless hands, as an ace reporter, getting the goods on the killer, played by John Barrymore.

In *Exposed* (1938), Glenda Farrell was a photographer (named "Click" Stewart) for a scandal magazine. She took a picture of a bum who turned out to be a disgraced lawyer, and then helped him to round up some racketeers who had caused his downfall.

Scandal Street, the same year, had to do with small-town gossips making life hell for Louise Campbell because of her relationship with a murdered roue. Helping to clear her

Scandal Street. Two popular reporters, Lew Ayres and Roscoe Karns, flank Louise Campbell. (Paramount, 1938)

*Ed Sullivan had already made his movie debut, playing himself in *Mr. Broadway,* in 1933.

60

besmirched name were veteran movie newsmen Lew Ayres and Roscoe Karns.

Other scandal-and-crime newspaper movies of the time included *Women Are Trouble* (1936), with Stuart Erwin, Paul Kelly and Florence Rice; *Framed* (1939), with Frank Albertson as the newshawk facing a phony murder rap; and *Sued for Libel* (1940), in which Kent Taylor, minus his familiar pencil-line mustache, had to uncover some killers in order to cancel out the unjust libel suit.

But scandalmonger movies had long since taken a new and refreshing twist, starting with a Frank Capra exercise in 1934 that was to set a new style in newspaper films as surely as

Women Are Trouble. A glum Stuart Erwin pays off a bet to his editor, Paul Kelly. (MGM, 1936)

Framed. Newsman Frank Albertson, between Jerome Cowan and Constance Moore. (Universal, 1939)

61

Sued for Libel. Linda Hayes and Kent Taylor led the cast of this press melodrama. (RKO, 1940)

Hecht and MacArthur had done with *The Front Page.*

The movie was the justly famous *It Happened One Night,* with down-at-the-heels newsman Clark Gable encountering runaway heiress Claudette Colbert. As their breezy romance blossoms, she is unaware that Gable is sending back stories about her to his newspaper. In the capable hands of director Capra (and writer Robert Riskin) it was a kind of updated *Taming of the Shrew,* and the film and all its principals walked off with Oscars the following spring.

(The framework was solid enough to stand two subsequent remakes, though neither one approached the style, wit, or box-office success of the original. In 1945, Ann Miller and

It Happened One Night. Reporter Clark Gable and runaway heiress Claudette Colbert thumb a ride in this scene from the smash-hit Capra film. (Columbia, 1934)

Eve Knew Her Apples. William Wright (at left) and Ann Miller were newsman and heiress in this later remake. (Columbia, 1945)

William Wright played the leads in a remake titled *Eve Knew Her Apples.* And in 1956, June Allyson was the heiress and Jack Lemmon the newshawk in a third version titled *You Can't Run Away from It.)*

You Can't Run Away from It. The third time around for *It Happened One Night.* The leads were June Allyson and Jack Lemmon. (Columbia, 1956)

Unlike many of the movies mentioned so far in this chapter, *It Happened One Night* was definitely an A picture, conceived by Capra and Riskin, ably executed by them, adeptly played by Colbert and Gable. Its success not only helped to raise the level of scandal newspaper films, but also paved the way for other first-rate films to come. For the remainder of the 1930s, the scandal newspaper movie genre continued to yield one or two good movies a year, some of them almost up to the level of *It Happened One Night,* one or two as good or better. In many of these, the scandal aspect was blurred somewhat, with the romance played up more. But the newspaperman had become an authentic American film hero, as appealing as a musketeer or a western marshal. And he seemed to be as welcome whether he was fighting crime or digging up scandal.

Miss Colbert, who had already been in several newspaper films even before the smash hit with Gable (with Norman Foster in *Young Man of Manhattan,* with Ben Lyon in *I Cover the Waterfront),* was now teamed with a new leading man, Fred MacMurray, in what was to mark the start of a busy film-newspaperman career for him.

This was a Wesley Ruggles comedy, *The Gilded Lily* (1935), in which MacMurray was a reporter and Claudette his girl. When a British peer (Ray Milland) proposes to her and she rejects him, MacMurray rushes to his typewriter, dubs her the "No Girl," and transforms her into a celebrity, all faster than you can say "Tear out the front page." After the usual bumps along the romantic road, Claudette decides to marry Fred.

Next was *The Bride Came Home,* also in 1935, again with Fred MacMurray, but this time with Robert Young instead of Ray Milland completing the triangle. Young and MacMurray were involved in starting a magazine, and wealthy Robert hired Claudette, your average penniless socialite, as an aide. After she agreed to marry Young, Fred chased after them (on a motorcycle) and convinced her it was him she really loved, after all.

If it seemed the newspaper connection was wearing thin, other studios had different

The Gilded Lily. Fred MacMurray, reporter, and
Claudette Colbert, his girlfriend, order something tall.
(Paramount, 1935)

The Bride Came Home. Fred MacMurray and
Claudette Colbert again in another newspaper yarn.
(Paramount, 1935)

Libeled Lady. William Powell was one of the stars of this, one of the best newspaper comedies of its time. (MGM, 1936)

ideas. In 1936, MGM came up with *Libeled Lady,* which turned out to be one of the slickest comedies of the year, with no less than four of the big studio's top stars involved: William Powell, Myrna Loy, Spencer Tracy, and Jean Harlow.

This time, the paper of which Tracy was editor was about to be sued for libeling heiress Myrna Loy. (There were a lot of heiresses around in movies in those days.) Tracy calls on Powell to figure out some way of stopping the suit. They work out a pretty devilish scheme: Powell is quietly married to Miss Harlow — she's really Tracy's fiancee but he temporarily sacrifices her to a higher cause — and then Powell is dispatched to meet and cultivate Miss Loy. He succeeds in this and she promptly falls in love with him. At this point, Tracy has it made: prepared to reveal that Powell is a married man, he is confident Miss Loy will cancel her libel suit. In the end,

of course, Loy and Powell pair off, as do Tracy and Harlow, and even though this comes as absolutly no surprise, there's enough fun along the way to make the film worthwhile.

Not quite as inventive, but still moderately successful, was *Love Is News* (1937) from 20th Century-Fox. This time, Loretta Young was the heiress and Tyrone Power the snoopy reporter who kept hounding her. To teach him a lesson — presumably about how unpleasant it is to live in the constant glare of publicity — Miss Young married the scandal-seeking reporter. The ending was more love than news.*

Also in 1937, one of the wittiest and most biting satires on the excesses of the press came along, once more from the brain of Ben Hecht, that most cynical of all ex-reporters. The film, deftly directed by William Wellman, was titled *Nothing Sacred* and starred Fredric March and Carole Lombard.

Reporter March and his editor (Walter Connolly) "discovered" Miss Lombard in a small Vermont town, where it had been reported she was a victim of radium poisoning, with only six weeks to live.

The two press opportunists promptly adopted her and hustled her to New York, to turn her into a celebrity—a shining example of bravery in the face of tragedy, and, incidentally, a sure circulation builder for their paper. In the midst of all the hoopla, Miss Lombard learned that the diagnosis of her fatal disease was wrong, but by then it was too late to stop the carnival. Some remember *Nothing Sacred* for the knock-down-drag-out fight between March and Lombard. But it's really the sharp Hecht dialogue, capably delivered by the stars, plus Hecht's heretical treatment of his alma mater, that made it such a rousing success.

(The character played by Miss Lombard, incidentally, was named Hazel Flagg. Some sixteen years later that was the title of a Broadway musical based on *Nothing Sacred.* And a year later, in 1954, the framework was used as the basis of a Dean Martin and Jerry

---

*In 1941, Republic made its own cheapie version, called *Public Enemies,* with Phillip Terry as the reporter and Wendy Barrie as the heiress.

Love Is News. Dudley Digges, Loretta Young, and
Tyrone Power. He was the news snoop, she the heiress.
(20th Century-Fox, 1937)

Nothing Sacred. One of the wittiest of all press movies
had Fredric March, (above) and Carole Lombard. With
March here is Troy Brown. (Selznick International,
1937)

Living It Up. Dean Martin and Jerry Lewis, with Janet Leigh, romped through this one, loosely based on *Nothing Sacred*. (Paramount, 1954)

Lewis comedy called *Living It Up*. Lewis was the supposedly dying innocent, and Janet Leigh the reporter assigned to exploit him. Clearly, Ben Hecht had no hand in this version.)

Fredric March got another crack at scandalmongering in 1938. This was in *There Goes My Heart*, yet one more reworking of the runaway heiress and the snoopy reporter. The heiress this time was cool Virginia Bruce, but the movie simply wasn't in the same class with *Nothing Sacred*.

In 1939, Fred Mac Murray played his fourth reporter role in *Café Society*, this time with Madeleine Carroll as his leading lady. He was a ship news reporter and she was a socialite who married him, to win a bet. Thin though it sounds, the film had its share of amusing moments, some of them supplied by Allyn Joslyn, playing a kind of take-off on Lucius Beebe, a society columnist of the time.

The scandal story with romantic overtones—or, perhaps, the romantic story with a scandal in the background—hit another peak in 1940 with the production of the memorable Katharine Hepburn-Cary Grant

There Goes My Heart. Fredric March, surrounded by Patsy Kelly and Virginia Bruce, was the reporter chasing the heiress. (United Artists, 1938)

Café Society. Ship news reporter Fred MacMurray and socialite Madeleine Carroll were in this comedy. (Paramount, 1939)

Café Society. Allyn Joslyn (left) played a snobbish society columnist. With him is Don Alvarado. (Paramount, 1939)

The Philadelphia Story. Socialite Katharine Hepburn faces scandal magazine representatives James Stewart and Ruth Hussey in this great comedy. (MGM, 1940)

film, *The Philadelphia Story*. Once again, the source material was the Broadway stage. Philip Barry wrote (reportedly at Hepburn's request) a play about a socialite on the verge of entering a second marriage. Because of some embarrassing skeletons, the snooty family is forced to endure the presence at the wedding of a scandal-magazine reporter and his female photographer. To further complicate matters, the young lady's first husband shows up unannounced. By the time all the dust has settled, the scandal writer has fallen (briefly) in love with the socialite, and she ends up giving her stuffy groom-to-be the air and returns to her first spouse.

Hepburn and Grant were both fine as Tracy Lord and G.K. Dexter Haven, but it was James Stewart as the reporter (paired with photographer Ruth Hussey) who walked off with the acting honors. Perhaps because he'd just missed an Oscar the year before (for *Mr. Smith Goes to Washington*) Stewart got one for *The Philadelphia Story*.

In 1949, Tyrone Power did a remake of his own earlier movie, *Love Is News*. This time, Gene Tierney was the heiress (instead of Loretta Young) and Power was still the snoopy reporter. The new version was called *That Wonderful Urge*, and again the socialite married the reporter to teach him a lesson (?), but somehow none of it seemed as amusing as it had back in the mid-1930s.

Even less amusing was a whimsical film Power had made the year before, called *The*

That Wonderful Urge. This version of *Love Is News* had Tyrone Power repeating his role, with Gene Tierney as the heiress. (20th Century-Fox, 1949)

Luck of the Irish (1948). Power played a newsman torn between his boss's daughter (Jayne Meadows) and an Irish colleen (Anne Baxter).

The boy-looking-for-scandal-meets-girl-on-the-run theme was splendidly revamped in 1953 by producer-director William Wyler in an irresistible confection called *Roman Holiday,* with Gregory Peck and Audrey Hepburn in the leading roles.

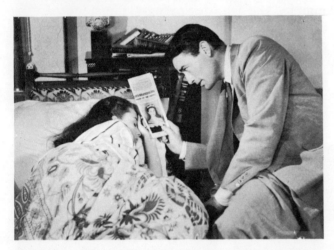

Roman Holiday. Sleeping princess Audrey Hepburn doesn't know yet that friend Gregory Peck is a reporter. (Paramount, 1953)

This time the young lady was a Ruritanian princess in Rome, fed up with the regimentation of her life. So she merely took off, disappeared. Before long, she met Gregory Peck, an American reporter currently down on his luck. Peck, aware of her identity, showed her the town, and the time of her life, all the while with his sidekick, photographer Eddie Albert, sneaking pictures for a proposed exclusive story-with-pictures about the missing princess's Roman spree.

Of course, Peck ended up turning soft, fell for the lovely young princess, and philosophically threw away his scoop rather than subject her to the embarrassment of a scandalous story. However unlikely that may seem, it was an appropriate enough ending for this pleasant fairy tale. (If the film had been made in the 1930s, he probably would have married the princess, which would be even more unlikely.)

Possibly as a result of the success of *Roman Holiday* (or, more probably, because MGM still owned the rights to *The Philadelphia Story*) in 1956 there was a new version of the Philip Barry play, this time all dressed up with some Cole Porter songs, and starring Grace Kelly as the socialite, Bing Crosby as the ex-husband, Frank Sinatra (of all people) as the snoopy reporter, and Celeste Holm as his charming photographer. The new title was *High Society,* and although it was a pleasant enough musical romp it lacked the bite of the original movie.

Meanwhile, the A-minus and B and even B-minus films went on and on. Before descending into the B category, George Brent made a second newspaper film with Bette Davis that must be regarded as an A if only because Davis and Brent were popular stars at the time.

The movie was *The Golden Arrow* (1936) and it had more twists than an E. Phillips Oppenheim spy novel. Davis was the madcap heiress whose every escapade made headlines. Only she was really an ex-cashier hired to pose as an heiress to help publicize a cosmetics firm. Brent was the sharp New York reporter sent to Florida to interview Davis when it is rumored she is about to marry a count. In no time at all, the count is forgotten and Davis marries Brent. There's a lot of nonsense about Brent getting drunk, being jailed and released in her custody, etc. but in the end he finds out she's really no heiress and, with typical Hollywood logic, this makes everything fine again.

Another 1936 B picture touching on scandal-plus-crime, but with less emphasis on romance, was *Exclusive Story,* with Franchot Tone as a special prosecutor and Stuart Erwin as the reporter helping him in his racket busting endeavors. Madge Evans was the leading lady.

In 1939, both Robert Cummings and Ray Milland were reporters in a Sonja Henie movie titled *Everything Happens at Night.* In this exercise, Miss Henie's father was an anti-Nazi intellectual, a Peace Prize winner reported dead but actually hiding from the Nazis

High Society. Frank Sinatra and Grace Kelly were among the stars in this musical based on *The Philadelphia Story.* (MGM, 1956)

The Golden Arrow. George Brent, a reporter again, with Eugene Pallette and Carol Hughes. (Warner Brothers, 1936)

Exclusive Story. Madge Evans talks with newsman Stuart Erwin while Franchot Tone watches. (MGM, 1936)

in Switzerland. Rival newshounds Cummings and Milland play cat-and-mouse games, each trying to convince the other he's not after a story, each trying to cultivate Miss Henie and thus locate her father. At one point, Milland swipes Cummings's story at the local telegraph office and sends it to his own paper. As for Miss Henie, she does some ice skating and a lot of giggling. In the end, Papa is rescued, Milland gets the story and Cummings gets Sonja.

Rosalind Russell, then Hollywood's most versatile career woman, was a judge in *Design for Scandal* (1941) and Walter Pidgeon was the reporter out to smear her good name. But he couldn't, so he married her instead.

Also in 1941, politics and scandalmongering

Everything Happens at Night. Sonja Henie is romanced by reporter Robert Cummings. (20th Century-Fox, 1939)

Design for Scandal. Journalist Walter Pidgeon argues with Edward Arnold over publishing some morsel of gossip. (MGM, 1941)

were mixed in *Washington Melodrama,* which had Frank Morgan as a congressman at loose ends, Kent Taylor as a snoopy reporter, and Ann Rutherford for romantic interest.

Two years later, Rosalind Russell was an author's agent in *What a Woman* (1943) and Brian Aherne was a magazine writer assigned to do a profile on her, and, naturally, hating the assignment. Once again, the romance pretty well blocked out the news angle.

Miss Russell, however, wasn't the only Hollywood star playing career women. Joan Crawford played her share of them, only hers tended to be rather humorless. One of them deserves mention here. It was a 1942 comedy called *They All Kissed the Bride,* with Miss Crawford as the hard-as-nails head of a trucking business and Melvyn Douglas as a cocky

Washington Melodrama. Kent Taylor is assaulted by Ann Rutherford right in the newsroom. (MGM, 1941)

What a Woman. Brian Aherne throws dice for the
drinks, while Willard Parker daydreams. The waiter is
Ferris Taylor. (Columbia, 1943)

They All Kissed the Bride. Joan Crawford has reporter
Melvyn Douglas thrown out by butler Roland Young
and strongman Ed Gargan. (Columbia, 1943)

newspaper reporter who blasts her in print for her arrogant business dealings. Joan gradually melts under the Douglas charm, becomes a Real Woman, and, thus, acceptable to Douglas.

Despite all these frothy love stories masquerading as newspaper yarns, the "real" scandal movies continued to come along, from time to time, throughout the 1950s and well into the 1960s. (For a time, there was a steady train of geographically oriented films about cities, possibly sparked by the popularity of such scandal magazines as *Confidential*. We had movies called *New York Confidential, Chicago Confidential, Miami Expose, Portland Expose, The Las Vegas Story, The Houston Story, The Phoenix City Story, etc.*, but these were mostly crime-busting yarns, with newspapermen only peripherally involved, if at all.)

Over-Exposed. Reporter Richard Crenna protects Cleo Moore in this melodrama. (Columbia, 1956)

Playgirl. Shelley Winters talks to a battery of reporters in this murder/news scandal film. (Universal-International, 1954)

In 1956, there was *Over-Exposed,* with Richard Crenna as a crime photographer who got the goods on a vice ring and ended up trading in his camera for a gun.

A scandal magazine was involved in *Playgirl* (1954) with Barry Sullivan as its publisher, Colleen Miller as a magazine cover girl, and Shelley Winters as her chum. Things get thick (and hokey) when Sullivan is found dead and the newspapers go after the story.

In 1957, Van Johnson played a television star whose career was jeopardized by an unscrupulous publisher of a scandal magazine (Steve Cochran) who got his kicks—and his profits—by blackmailing celebrities with imperfect pasts. The film was called *Slander.*

Secret File Hollywood (1962) was about the bottom of the barrel. Robert Clarke and Francine York were the principals in this minor entry that dealt with vice racketeers and scandal magazines.

And in 1965 there was what might be termed an "A-double-minus" called *Sex and the Single Girl.* Only the title of Helen Gurley Brown's book remained in this production, with Natalie Wood playing a research psychologist and Tony Curtis as a scandal-magazine reporter. What people like Lauren Bacall, Henry Fonda, and Mel Ferrer were doing in the cast, one can only wonder.

But the scandalmonger romance movie had long since run its course. Over the years it had reached such highs as *It Happened One Night, Nothing Sacred,* and *Roman Holiday*

Slander. Slime publisher Steve Cochran is about to ruin
Van Johnson's career in this movie. (MGM, 1957)

Secret File Hollywood. Francine York and Robert Clarke were the principals in this scandal flick. (Crown International, 1962)

Sex and the Single Girl. Tony Curtis was the scandal-monger and Natalie Wood his quarry. (Warner Brothers, 1965)

and such lows as *Scandal Street, Exposed,* and *Over-Exposed.* As to why the scandal movie finally fizzled, a number of reasons might be advanced, but perhaps the least de-pressing to contemplate is that reporters in films had found far greener fields in which to operate.

THE REPORTER AS CRUSADER

4

Whenever anyone tries to defend Hollywood against the sweeping charge that all its studios have ever turned out have been idiotic beach-party musicals and mock-horror Vincent Price movies, the handiest ammunition has often been the string of "socially aware" or "message" pictures made over the years.

Hollywood has taken justifiable pride in films that have exposed social evils, with whatever degree of artistic and/or financial success. The list is impressive enough—from *I Am a Fugitive from a Chain Gang* (1932), which threw a harsh light on miserable prison conditions, and *The Grapes of Wrath* 1940), which displayed compassion for the poverty-stricken and disenfranchised Okies, to *Twelve Angry Men* (1957), which explored bigotry among jurors, and *Serpico* (1973), an exposé of police corruption.

Among the many others have been *Confessions of a Nazi Spy* (1939), *Dr. Ehrlich's Magic Bullet* (1940), *Mr. Smith Goes to Washington* (1939), *The Best Years of Our Lives* (1946), *The Diary of Anne Frank* (1959), *The Ox Bow Incident* (1943), *On the Waterfront* (1954), *The Snake Pit* (1949), and *On the Beach* (1959). These dealt with the Nazi menace, fighting venereal diseases, political corruption, the problems of returning veterans, the plight of European Jews, lynching, labor racketeering, the treatment of mental patients, and the horrors of atomic war. Obviously, anyone can make up his own list of "important" films, meaning films that have dealt seriously with serious issues.

Just as in real life newspapers and news-papermen have often performed worthwhile functions in their communities, Hollywood films have sometimes told stories of just such newspapers and their reporters. Of course, as with other films, the intention has sometimes been better than the result. Nevertheless, Hollywood movies about newspaper life have sometimes reached their highest levels in stories about crusading newsmen.

From the earliest days of talking films, Warner Brothers took pride in its social-message movies, which included *I Am a Fugitive from a Chain Gang, The Life of Emile Zola, Watch on the Rhine,* and others. The same studio, it is true, tried to cloak its sensational gangster films in respectability, usually by showing graphically that "crime doesn't pay." But often the hoods were shown as glamorous types, and even their bloody demise at the end couldn't wipe out the appealing images created by Robinson, Cagney, Bogart, and other Warner Brothers movie gangsters.

Having delved successfully into chain-gang conditions, in the 1932 Paul Muni film, the studio had another go at the same subject, with variations, in *Road Gang* (1936). But this time the hero was a news reporter, Donald Woods, whose troubles started when he began writing a series of articles exposing corrupt politicians. A trumped up charge lands Woods on the chain gang, then to a convicts' road gang sent to work in the mines. Eventually, the convict miners riot and escort Woods to a district attorney, where, presumably, action to punish the grafting politicians and improve

Road Gang. Donald Woods, a reporter in disguise, embraces Kay Linaker now that his crusade has been won. (Warner Brothers, 1936)

conditions on the chain gangs will be forthcoming.

Compared to the earlier Muni effort (or almost anything else) *Road Gang* was decidedly a B picture, despite a script by onetime newspaperman Dalton Trumbo, then and for many years later one of Hollywood's best writers.

In 1939, also from Warner Brothers, came *Each Dawn I Die,* one of a rash of prison pictures turned out by that studio. But this one involved a crusading newsman (James Cagney) who was hot on the trail of a political scandal when he was framed on a phony manslaughter charge and sent to prison. There he was befriended by hardened criminal George Raft, who offered to work for Cagney's release if Cagney would help Raft escape. At

first, the reporter spurned the offer, but a taste of tough prison life changed his mind. The story, full of twists, turns, and action, ended with Raft sacrificing himself during a prison-break attempt, but clearing Cagney's good name.

Each Dawn I Die was based on a story by Jerome Odlum, once the managing editor of a Minneapolis newspaper, and also the author of *Nine Lives Are Not Enough* (1941), mentioned in an earlier chapter.

Frank Capra, whose *It Happened One Night* triggered a whole series of newspaperman-chasing-heiress films, used crusading newspaper reporters at two levels in *Mr. Smith Goes to Washington* which was really about an honest young politician beat-

Each Dawn I Die. Crusading reporter James Cagney was framed (knocked out, placed in a car, whiskey poured over him) to prevent him from exposing corruption. But he managed to get his scoop in the end. (Warner Brothers, 1939)

Mr. Smith Goes to Washington. Jean Arthur had newsman Thomas Mitchell on her side in this political drama. (Columbia, 1939)

ing the odds. Mr. Smith was played to perfection by James Stewart, and Jean Arthur was his worldly-wise secretary, sadly watching him being duped by such evil politicos as Claude Rains, Edward Arnold, and Guy Kibbee.

But reporter Thomas Mitchell, who has a crush on Miss Arthur himself, pitches in to help the embattled young senator. And when the powerful Arnold pressures the newspapers in Stewart's home state to make no mention of the senator's brave fillibuster, Stewart's mother (Beulah Bondi) organizes the boys whose scoutmaster Stewart had been to put out and distribute their own little paper, to let people know what's going on in Washington. Capra even tossed in radio commentator H.V. Kaltenborn, appearing as himself and commenting on Mr. Smith's heroic fight, to add a touch of authenticity to the film. All in all, it was a splendid movie, a paean to democracy that, peripherally, at least, stressed the importance of a free press.

Having enjoyed much critical success with films about such worthy gentlemen as Louis Pasteur and Emile Zola (both played by Paul Muni) and Dr. Ehrlich (Edward G. Robinson), Warners next cast Robinson as Julius Reuter in the 1940 movie, *A Dispatch from Reuter's*. This was essentially the story of how that famed news agency began, somewhat fanciful and not altogether gripping. Still, it was interesting enough to see Reuter sending off carrier pigeons with hot news stories across the English Channel. One might argue that Reuter was more concerned with launching a successful business than with informing the world of important events, but, then, that argument could conceivably be used against Pulitzer, Hearst, Luce, or Sulzberger.

The year 1942 marked the beginning of the highly successful teaming of Katharine Hepburn and Spencer Tracy. One of their eight films together involved a kind of crusading journalist and the widow of a public hero. The film was titled *Keeper of the Flame* (1942), and

A Dispatch from Reuter's. Eddie Albert watches Edward G. Robinson send off a scoop, via carrier pigeon. (Warner Brothers, 1940)

Keeper of the Flame. Spencer Tracy and Audrey Christie were both reporters in this heavy drama. (MGM, 1942)

it was notable not only for good performances but also for an air of mystery that helped sustain interest in a rather gloomy story.

Tracy played a noted journalist out to do a biography of a revered man who had been killed when his car went off a bridge. The man's widow (Miss Hepburn) has avoided interviews but agrees to talk to Tracy when he tells her how much he admired her late husband. In time, Tracy learns that the widow could have prevented the man's death: it seems she knew about the bridge being broken. Badgered by Tracy, she finally confesses that she let her husband die because he was secretly a fascist who planned to use his great popularity to catapult himself into a dictator's position. Somewhat shattered, Tracy agrees to suppress the story rather than let the American public know what a fraud the dead man had really been. But when the widow herself dies, Tracy prints the full story, exposing the phony hero.

A crusading journalist of more familiar stripe was James Cagney in the 1943 film,

Johnny Come Lately. Roving newsman James Cagney came to the aid of elderly publisher Grace George. (United Artists, 1943)

Johnny Come Lately. Cagney played an itinerant reporter a little down on his luck, who just happens to wander into a town where his services are sorely needed. Seems a kindly old biddy (played by Grace George) has been trying to keep her small-town newspaper healthy and honest—frequently, it would appear, a difficult combination—but just isn't capable of taking on the assortment of crooks and two-faced politicians who oppose her. So, Cagney writes to the rescue, saves the paper, drives out the rascals, and, in the process, gives his own self-respect a much needed boost. It was a fairly palatable, if not especially distinguished, film.

The crusading journalist—and never mind what he was crusading for—had by now become a recognizable and generally admired screen figure. Such an identity was sometimes tagged onto a central character quite irrelevantly, almost as if some producer were deciding whether the hero mightn't look a little better with a mustache. For example, another film from Warners was *One More Tomorrow* (1946), with Ann Sheridan, Dennis Morgan, and Alexis Smith. This was really a romantic comedy with nice girl Sheridan and icy bitch Smith both pursuing playboy Morgan. Almost as an after-thought, Morgan was called upon to run a "liberal" magazine, possibly because such a humanitarian activity would tend to soften the fact that he was rich, reckless, and occasionally drunk.

A far more admirable crusading journalist

One More Tomorrow. Ann Sheridan dines with magazine editor and playboy Dennis Morgan. (Warner Brothers, 1946)

Gentlemen's Agreement. Crusading journalist Gregory Peck examined anti-Semitism in this fine film. With him above is Nicholas Joy. (20th Century-Fox, 1947)

was Gregory Peck in the 1947 movie, *Gentlemen's Agreement.* Taken from the Laura Z. Hobson best-selling book, this excellent film examined anti-Semitism—from the vicious to the casual—as writer Peck went about posing as a Jew in order to find out how much discrimination he'd encounter. To the shock and dismay of far too many people who should have known better, he encountered quite a bit of it.

But the Elia Kazan film was pursuasively made, and somehow Peck didn't seem either condescending or artificial in his battle against this particular brand of racial bigotry. It was named best picture of the year, and both Kazan and actress Celeste Holm, in a supporting role, won Oscars.

The following year, 1948, the same studio (20th Century-Fox) gave us another first-rate crusading journalist, although this time the focal point was back to crime. Despite that, the movie, called *Call Northside 777,* stands up as one of the best newspaper films made. Its leading character, James Stewart, was not that familiar figure, the wise-cracking reporter who outsmarts the cops and hurls insults at his editors.

Instead, he was a plodding, serious newsman who gradually comes to believe in the innocence of a man already in jail for some

Call Northside 777. Kasia Orzazewski asks reporter James Stewart's help in proving her son's innocence. (20th Century-Fox, 1948)

In the end, it was another character, a somewhat crazed doctor (Shepperd Strudwick) who killed the arrogant politician, leaving us to wonder whether the reporter wasn't somehow relieved to have the demagogue done in, yet without blood on his own hands. If only by implication, the film also served to point up a pitfall to journalists covering political affairs: the closer a reporter gets to the center of power, the less able he is to maintain his independent position as a representative of the press.

But if Broderick Crawford wasn't defeated by a reporter in that film, he certainly was in his next big picture. This was the brilliant Garson Kanin comedy, *Born Yesterday* (1950), and once again the reporter got somebody else to do the dirty work.

This delightful fable introduced us to Harry Brock (Crawford), a bully of a junk dealer who has come to Washington to "buy" a senator. He is accompanied by Billie Dawn (Judy Holliday) and to this day it is difficult to know who

eleven years. Perhaps because it was based on a true story—or, more likely, because the director and writers had enough faith in the original story to avoid rewriting it to death—much of the film rang true, from Stewart's portrayal of the hard-digging reporter, to Lee J. Cobb's as the dubious editor, to Richard Conte's as the man wrongly convicted. It proved, too, that good, suspenseful newspaper stories could be made (and accepted by the public) without comic copy boys, hysterical editors, or loud-mouthed crime busters yelling, "Stop the presses!"

The early 1950s were to become what might be regarded as the Golden Age of the crusading journalist in movies. Perhaps the trend was hinted at in 1949 with Robert Rossen's fine screen version of the Robert Penn Warren book, *All the King's Men*. This dealt with the rise and fall of a demagogue, brilliantly played by Broderick Crawford. Not central to the main story, but giving the audience a kind of vantage point from which to assess the proceedings, was the role assigned John Ireland. He played a newspaperman, though not quite a crusader; instead, he was an observer who rode on Crawford's coattails, chronicling the politician's rise to prominence, then gradually getting sucked into the political inner circle, eventually writing the demagogue's speeches.

All the King's Men. Reporter John Ireland chronicled the rise of a demagogue, but couldn't remain aloof. (Columbia, 1949)

85

Born Yesterday. Washington reporter William Holden
first coached then fell for Judy Holliday. (Columbia,
1950)

was more wonderful—the character or the actress. Billie was the docile doxie, kept handy to sign incomprehensible papers, unwitting aid in Brock's complex dummy corporation and nefarious dealings.

Enter William Holden, the incorruptible Washington journalist, already suspicious of Crawford and out to expose him as a menace. Crawford turns Miss Holliday over to Holden to "educate" her. And how he educates her. By the time Holden is through with her, she not only has become dimly aware of how much nicer Holden is than Crawford, but she has a fine appreciation of what democracy is all about and what a threat to it Crawford represents. *Born Yesterday* was a classic example of how to make a fairly serious pill

(preaching about democracy) taste thoroughly delicious.

In the late 1940s and early 1950s, Hollywood was very much aware of Washington. It was the time of the House Un-American Activities Committee, a group that descended on the movie industry like a vigilante mob, leaving in their wake many ruined careers and a legacy of fear that was to last for more than a decade. The postwar fear of communism, so effectively exploited by Senator Joseph McCarthy and other ambitious politicians (including, incidentally, a California congressman named Richard Nixon), had a tendency to diminish any producer's enthusiasm for making movies about corrupt politicians and powerful businessmen who could manipulate them. Frank Capra's Mr. Smith, so appealing in 1939, would surely have been drummed out of Washington (on film, at least) by 1949. More to the public's liking—or so rationalized Hollywood, anyway—were films like *The Iron Curtain*, about Soviet spies operating in Canada, or *My Son, John*, about a "suspicious" unpatriotic American who sits around reading books instead of playing football. Naturally, he turns out to be a communist agent.

But not all the news from Washington was untouchable. There was also Senator Estes Kefauver, who made a national name for himself by investigating organized crime. His attention-getting activities inspired more than one movie, and sometimes the combination of fearless special investigator and crusading journalist worked, in the movies, at least.

One of these was *The Turning Point* (1952), with William Holden as the hard-boiled journalist and Edmond O'Brien as the idealistic public investigator dedicated to exposing the crime syndicate in his city. By way of a switch, Holden discovered that O'Brien's policeman father (Tom Tully) was himself involved in the rackets. Holden softens enough to withhold this knowledge from his pal, O'Brien, but later O'Brien takes even this blow in his stride and goes right on tracking down the racketeers. Holden, meanwhile, shifts gradually from cynic to crusader and eventually turns martyr—inevitably stepping over that boundary that separates real-life newsmen from movie journalists and going after the crooks himself—and ends up dying heroically.

Far more convincing, even though it was a

The Turning Point. William Holden was a crusading newsman with worries galore in this melodrama. (Paramount, 1952)

Captive City. Fighting editor John Forsythe and his wife, Joan Camden, were terrorized by mobsters. (United Artists, 1952)

B picture (in terms of budget, at any rate), was *Captive City* (also made in 1952), with John Forsythe as the sole "name" in the cast.

Forsythe was the editor and part-owner of a newspaper in a medium-sized city. A local citizen seeks his support in exposing "the syndicate," and after Forsythe dismisses him as a crackpot, the man is run down by a car and killed. Gradually coming to believe the poor man was onto something, Forsythe starts needling the police in print for their inaction (in failing to find who ran down the man) and in turn finds himself being harassed. The more Forsythe digs, the more dirt he finds, and the more thorny his task becomes.

Even when he has reason to suspect that the "harmless" gambling the police allow is actually being run by Mafia representatives (and, unlike later films, the word "Mafia" was used here), Forsythe finds himself unable to get any help. When he writes an open letter to the police, offering his evidence, his own partner in the newspaper refuses to run it and tries to buy Forsythe out.

Forsythe, whose own wife (Joan Camden) is beginning to suspect he's tilting at windmills, calls together the city's clergymen. They give him lip service but he gradually realizes, to his horror, that they won't back him up because their well-to-do congregations want the gambling in the town to continue.

By now, the crusading journalist finds him-self in the classic High Noon situation: the town he is fighting to clean up has turned against him for making waves. Finally, with his own life in danger, Forsythe and his wife decide to go straight to the Kefauver Committee. The film ends with the journalist and his wife arriving safely at the building where the crime investigating committee is meeting. There is a preachy tag in which Senator Kefauver himself appears, praising this "outstanding member of his profession" and urging other citizens to speak out and help defeat organized crime.

What made *Captive City* so good was its air of authenticity. Director Robert Wise managed to steer clear of almost all the standard newspaper movie clichés, presenting his story in tight, semidocumentary style that helped make it that much more convincing. In addition, he even managed to touch on the sometimes conflicting interests of the news-gathering and advertising departments within a newspaper.

Certainly, *Captive City* was more believable than either *The Turning Point* or another 1952 film about a crusading journalist. This was *The Sell-Out,* with Walter Pidgeon using his newspaper to root out corruption in his city's law enforcement. This time John Hodiak was the state's attorney, and — re-

The Sell-Out. Everett Sloane, Walter Pidgeon, and Cameron Mitchell (seated) were the principals in this one. (MGM, 1952)

miniscent of *The Turning Point* — Pidgeon discovered that his own son-in-law (Cameron Mitchell) was involved with the crooks.

Still less memorable was *Operation X,* released in 1950, with Edward G. Robinson as a sort of ruthless tycoon out to rule the world and Richard Greene as the crusading young journalist quietly investigating Robinson. But the story really had to do with Robinson's obsessive love for his daughter, played by Peggy Cummins. Greene was aboard mostly to provide a sturdy shoulder for Miss Cummins to lean on.

Now and then, the world of westerns would pay a little lip (or gun) service to freedom of the press. One would think such a subject,

against the vast backdrop of the opening of the West, would yield some stirring yarns. However, few such major films came along, and those that did tended to skim over the subject, as in the Errol Flynn actioner *Dodge City* (1939), in which the local editor of this famous frontier town (Frank McHugh) is just one more corpse among many gunned down by the black hats.

In 1941, that intrepid lawman, Hopalong Cassidy (William Boyd) came down hard on the side of a free press in *Wide Open Town,* helping a harassed editor (Morris Ankrum) rid the community of outlaws.

Randolph Scott, another perennial hero of mostly small-budget westerns, went further.

Operation X. Reporter Richard Greene confronts Edward G. Robinson, as Finlay Currie looks on. (Columbia, 1950)

Dodge City. Errol Flynn captures Bruce Cabot. At
extreme left is Frank McHugh, the local editor. At
right, Alan Hale. (Warner Brothers, 1939)

Wide Open Town, William Boyd (as Hopalong Cassidy)
helped western editor Morris Ankrum (center) clean
out the outlaws. (Paramount, 1941)

Fort Worth. Editor Randolph Scott, with Dick Jones (at left) used his press until he had to use his gun. (Warner Brothers, 1951)

In *Fort Worth* (1951) he was the editor of a frontier newspaper who ultimately had to strap on his guns to clean up the town, suggesting that out west, at least, the gun was mightier than the pen.

And in *The San Francisco Story* (1952), Joel McCrea was a mining tycoon who joined forces with a newspaper crusader, and the vigilantes, to undo crook Sidney Blackmer.

Writer-producer-director Samuel Fuller deserves some separate attention here. His is the classic example of the true-life newspaperman who later dipped, again and again, into his background for source material. Once a copy boy to the legendary *New York Journal* editor, Arthur Brisbane, young Fuller was a hot-shot reporter when he was still in his late teens. Soon he was writing short stories and he sold his first movie script in 1936.

The San Francisco Story. Joel McCrea and Yvonne DeCarlo starred in this western, which involved some hanky-panky with the local paper. (Warner Brothers, 1952)

The Second World War interrupted his budding screen career, but after that he was back in Hollywood, writing and soon directing his own films. In recent years, a kind of cult has developed around Fuller (as with another maker of hard-hitting, small budget films, Don Siegel), and his more dedicated followers have found both philosophical viewpoint and cinematic style in his works.

Some of Fuller's newspaper-oriented films are dealt with in other chapters of this book, but two of them properly belong in the Crusader category.

His most serious work was *Park Row,* released by United Artists in 1952. It was serious partly because it was a labor of love for Fuller. *Park Row* was his first independent production, into which he reportedly put his own money, an unusual, not to say unique, action for film producers. (Somebody once defined a film producer as a man who shoots dice with someone else's money.)

Park Row. Attempting to capture authenticity, producer Sam Fuller issued an engraving with this scene still showing an early linotype machine. The editor (standing) is Gene Evans. (United Artists, 1952)

The ads for *Park Row* explained the title this way: "The street of rogues...reporters...and romance!" Actually, it is a street in downtown Manhattan once associated with newspaper publishing. Fuller's *Park Row* was an attempt to capture some of the excitement and romance of turn-of-the-century newspaper rivalry in New York. His protagonist, Phineas Mitchell (played by Gene Evans), is a rough-and tough reporter who gets fired for bucking the Establishment policies of his well-heeled lady publisher. So, naturally, he decides to start his own daily newspaper, an enterprise, one would think, no more daring or complex in those days than, say, starting another professional football team would be today. But Phineas is determined that his paper should stand for Truth and Integrity, fight social evils, expose corruption, defend little people, denounce injustice, and, almost incidentally, sell papers. Before too many scenes have gone by, history and dramatic license are in a life-and-death struggle for supremacy in the film's brisk direction.

Fuller's historical-biographical detail sometimes gets in the way of his dramatic sense, his flair for violent action. But although *Park Row* was no landmark in filmed newspaper history (as the earlier *Citizen Kane* was), it at least conveyed Fuller's grasp of the excitement of the world of the press in an era before he lived.

Eleven years later, Samuel Fuller went to the newspaper well again, with *Shock Corridor* (1963), with Peter Breck as a crusading journalist who enters a mental hospital (posing as a patient) to try to solve a murder. But by now it seemed as if Fuller had been too long away from the world of journalism, too long involved in the Hollywood world of sensational scenes. Once in the mental hospital, Breck encounters the kind of inmates one has come to expect in movie madhouses.

One is a Korean War veteran who thinks he is a Civil War general; obese Larry Tucker throws his overweight around; another fellow, brought up as a bigot, defected to the Communists, later changed his mind and was labeled mentally ill.

As for Breck, he has his own troubles. Supposedly a Pulitzer Prize winner, he begins to lose his marbles in this unhealthy atmosphere.

Shock Corridor. The man being dragged by two attendants is Peter Breck, playing a reporter on assignment in a mental hospital. (Allied Artists, 1963)

When he is finally told the name of the killer, he forgets it. (In *Park Row,* this would have gotten him fired.)

If, as his admirers claim, Fuller attempts to make a statement in his films, the statement here must be that seeking the truth in today's society will drive anyone mad. Even so, in *Shock Corridor,* journalism gets the Fuller brush.

The journalist as do-it-yourself crusader was effectively portrayed in a well-intentioned, if not altogether successful, 1964 movie, *Black Like Me,* starring James Whitmore. Based on the true experiences of writer John Howard Griffin, the film dealt graphi-

cally with the humiliations suffered by Griffin (Whitmore) when he posed as a black man and hitchhiked his way through the American South.

But the crusading journalist never got a better shake from Hollywood than he did in *Deadline, U.S.A.,* a 1952 Richard Brooks movie starring Humphrey Bogart. Indeed, the whole world of journalism was rarely depicted with as much understanding as this movie displayed.

Deadline, U.S.A. was made at a time when television was on its way up—not only as a medium of entertainment but as a source of news—and newspapers were beginning to ex-

Black Like Me. Crusading reporter James Whitmore posed as a black to do an exposé. (Walter Reade-Sterling, Inc., 1964)

Deadline, U.S.A. Humphrey Bogart was the most appealing of crusading journalists in this meticulously accurate story of the death of a newspaper. (20th Century-Fox, 1952)

perience the start of what has been a steady decline in a good many American cities in the two decades since.

The movie deals with the dying days of a big city newspaper and the effects of that imminent demise on the newsmen who work there. The paper is about to be sold to a rival paper (and then phased out) by the late owner's relatives. Only his widow (Ethel Barrymore) is sympathetic to Bogart's impassioned pleas to save the newspaper, but in the end even she is powerless to rescue the doomed paper.

Along the way, however, writer-director Brooks gives his characters some appealing and haunting things to say about the world of newspaper people.

"It's not our job," says managing editor

Bogart, talking about a racketeer, "to prove he's guilty. We're not detectives and we're not a law enforcement agency."

"A journalist," echoes reporter Jim Backus," makes himself the hero of a story; a reporter is just a witness."*

At a somewhat sentimental, but curiously affecting, wake for the paper, held at the nearby saloon, news hen Audrey Christie reflects wistfully on "The best fourteen years" of her life.

"And what have I got to show for it?" she continues. "Eighty-one dollars in the bank, two dead husbands and a few kids I never had. I've covered everything from electrocutions to love nest raids...And I never saw Paris."

Still later in the movie, Bogart advises a young journalism student: "So you wanna be a reporter? Here's a bit of advice. Don't ever change your mind. It may not be the oldest profession, but it's the best."

As a kind of epilogue, Bogart delivers an impassioned plea for the existence of competitive newspapers — "the market place of ideas."

But by then it's too late, both for the newspaper in the movie, and the movie itself. For all his grasp of the dedication of reporters to their work, Brooks has Bogart do an about-face and, despite his earlier argument, turn detective, prosecutor, and jury. The film is climaxed by a burst of violence as out of place as it is dated.

Once more, the requirements of film drama supersede the dictates of logic. But up to this point, it is a skillful, satisfying, and affecting movie. Hollywood has not often caught better the flavor of a newspaper office, nor more believably conveyed the role of crusading journalism in American life.

*American reporters have long considered the word *journalist* snobbish, except perhaps when refering to deceased colleagues.

5

THE REPORTER OVERSEAS

In the days when the sun never set on British soil, it was customary (in films, at least) to hear stiff-upper-lipped militarists facing up to trouble spots anywhere in the world with the simplistic solution of their time: "Send in a regiment and clean the beggars out."

Since, in those days, American involvement in global matters was somewhat more limited than it later became, the primary American need was to know what was going on, to learn the "inside" story, as ferreted out and interpreted by enterprising American reporters sent to the scene for that specific purpose. Hence, the American overseas correspondent, a figure glamorized by American movies neither more nor less than the homebound reporter.

Naturally, the foreign correspondent's life in film was more dramatic in time of war rather than peace. In fact, Hollywood didn't always wait around for a war to come along; it was simpler to cook one up to serve the purpose.

Thus, as early as 1932, we had *War Correspondent,* with Ralph Graves in the title role and Jack Holt as an American masquerading as a Chinese war lord. (Chinese war lords were very big in those days; they could be invented at any time to function as clay pigeons for bold American foreign correspondents to aim at.)

In 1934, Cecil B. DeMille, more noted for huge casts and spectacular productions, turned out *Four Frightened People,* in which William Gargan, as an American correspondent, and Claudette Colbert, as a prim librarian, are among the survivors of a shipwreck in the Pacific. It had overtones of *The Admirable Crichton,* with roving reporter Gargan emerging as the natural leader of the little lost band of travelers.

In the early 1930s, Lee Tracy, who had become pretty firmly established as the movie's most popular fast-talking reporter, tried his hand at overseas correspondence. In *Clear All Wires* (1933), Tracy was a brash foreign correspondent tangling with an assortment of sinister agents of unfriendly, but unnamed, foreign powers. (Another rule of the game in those days was that you didn't identify the unfriendly foreign power.) Wiry James Gleason was his aid, and Benita Hume played an English sob sister.

The following year, Tracy was again unscrambling various global problems. He located a lost dirigible, rescued a queen from assassination, and followed a revolution in *I'll Tell The World* (1934). This time, Roger Pryor, another B-picture reporter, played Tracy's rival.

Also in 1934, Lee Tracy was to have played a key role in a big MGM movie about Pancho Villa, titled *Viva Villa.* This had Wallace Beery in the title role, and Tracy was scheduled to play an American correspondent who befriended the famous Mexican rebel.

Ben Hecht, by now an old hand at delineating fascinating American newspaper reporters, wrote in a good part for Tracy. But the production on location in Mexico, ran into trouble when Tracy, apparently beginning to live his role of brash reporter, so offended the Mexican authorities that they ordered him de-

Four Frightened People. Claudette Colbert, Mary Boland, Herbert Marshall, and William Gargan represent the title. Gargan was the traveling journalist. (Paramount, 1934)

Clear All Wires. James Gleason offers encouragement while foreign correspondent Lee Tracy taps out his story. (MGM, 1933)

I'll Tell the World. Roger Pryor (left) was one of the glib foreign correspondents in this B picture. (Universal, 1934)

Viva Villa. Stuart Erwin, the roving reporter, tangles with Pancho Villa (Wallace Beery). The girl is Katherine DeMille. (MGM, 1934)

ported. (According to legend, drinking was the cause of it all.)

The role was changed somewhat and given to Stuart Erwin, an actor of less flamboyant style. Erwin got good reviews, as did the film, and if the American correspondent in this particular case didn't settle down the foreign villains single-handed, at least he was on the side of the folk-hero underdog.

The dilemma of a reporter assigned to go overseas at the risk of destroying his marriage was tackled in *Next Time We Love* (1936), with James Stewart as the newman and Margaret Sullavan as his ambitious actress wife. Eventually, the stage lost a budding actress when Stewart pursuaded her to accompany him on his globe-trotting assignments.

Love on the Run. Foreign correspondents Clark Gable and Franchot Tone were rivals for Joan Crawford, and the story. (MGM, 1936)

Next Time We Love. Margaret Sullavan and James Stewart starred in this marital drama. (Universal, 1936)

Fictional foreign intrigue was combined with romantic comedy in *Love on the Run* (1936), with Clark Gable, Joan Crawford, and Franchot Tone. Gable and Tone were rival overseas correspondents. In the course of battling over Crawford, they trip over a plot to steal British military secrets, and from there on in it's a multilevel chase film: reporters vying for a hot story, men competing for a woman, spies trying to stop everybody.

By the mid-1930's, American filmmakers were running out of wars to cover. *I Cover the War* (1937) had John Wayne as a newsreel cameraman on assignment in Mesopotamia, finding time enough to crush a totally imaginary Arab revolt.

And then came Generalissimo Francisco Franco. The first Hollywood movie to deal with the Spanish Civil War was called *Last Train from Madrid*. It was issued in 1937 and had a cast headed by Dorothy Lamour, Lew Ayres, and Gilbert Roland. Ayres was the flip American correspondent in the beleaguered Spanish metropolis, Miss Lamour was a kind of mystery woman linked with warrior Roland. Typically, the movie took no sides—that came later—but attempted to suggest that most obvious of all Hollywood themes: war is hell.

Before the Second World War was to absorb us all (including moviemakers) one really worthwhile film about a real-life globe-trotting reporter was made, in 1939. This was the 20th Century-Fox film, *Stanley and Livingstone,* with Spencer Tracy starring as the famous reporter who succeeded in locating the equally famous missing missionary.

Just as movie critics had, in the past, bristled at the wildly exaggerated portraits of newmen in countless hokey Hollywood films, the majority of them found much to admire in this drama, partly, one might conclude, because its protagonist was portrayed with taste, restraint and intelligence. The script was by ex-newsman Sam Hellman.

Last Train from Madrid. American correspondent Lew
Ayres meets Olympe Bradne in this melodrama about
Spain's Civil War. (Paramount, 1937)

Stanley and Livingstone. Editor Henry Hull assigns
reporter Spencer Tracy to find the famous missionary.
(20th Century-Fox, 1939)

Tracy played Henry M. Stanley, a veteran reporter for the *New York Herald*, who was assigned by his editor, James Gordon Bennett, Jr. (Henry Hull in the movie) to go to Africa in search of Dr. David Livingstone. Tracy's adventures, before he finds the missionary, are fascinating and suspenseful without plunging into the depths of B-picture melodrama.

But, Hollywood was still Hollywood, so we had to have a brush with romance (Stanley falls for Nancy Kelly, who prefers Richard Greene) and even a totally misleading denouement that has Stanley returning to the jungle to carry on Dr. Livingstone's missionary work.

In the wake of the tremendously successful *Ninotchka*, an Ernst Lubitsch comedy poking fun at Russian communism, Ben Hecht and Charles Lederer brought forth another bright comedy, *Comrade X,* in 1940, with Clark Gable as an American correspondent in Moscow.

Once again, it was an American view of the duplicity of communist rulers, but although it lacked the comic invention that distinguished the Lubitsch film, it had its moments, and both Gable and Hedy Lamarr were praised for their performances in the movie. Despite the emphasis on romantic comedy, and the inevitable digs at Russian tyranny, Gable was still an American foreign correspondent sneaking out stories attacking the Soviet regime.

By now, Hollywood had begun openly fight-

Comrade X. Overseas reporter Clark Gable meets Moscow's most glamorous streetcar conductor, Hedy Lamarr. (MGM, 1940)

101

Foreign Correspondent. Joel McCrea puts a protective
arm about Larraine Day in this exciting moment of the
Hitchcock film. (United Artists, 1940)

ing the Nazis, before the United States was in
the war, and also openly needling the Rus-
sians, who were temporarily allied with
Hitler's Germany.

But it took Alfred Hitchcock to turn out the
first and certainly the best of the Second
World War movies about overseas correspondents. The movie, still regarded by some
as Hitchcock's best American-made film, was
named *Foreign Correspondent* and had Joel
McCrea in the title role, with Larraine Day,
Herbert Marshall, George Sanders, Robert
Benchley, and Albert Basserman in the supporting cast.

(Remarkably, the film's credits claim the
film was based on *Personal History* by Vincent Sheean. That fine book was published a

full five years earlier, well before anything
resembling war clouds began to gather over
Europe.)

Perhaps sensing American confusion over
conflicting reports about what was really
going on in Europe in the late 1930s, Hitchcock began with a crusty old newspaper editor
(Harry Davenport) expressing his impatience
with the mumbo-jumbo of jaded foreign correspondents. "I want a good, honest crime
reporter," he says, and, virtually on cue, in
walks young Joel McCrea, a cub reporter
about to be fired for tangling with the New
York police.

The publisher/editor promptly appoints
McCrea to go to Europe, changing the young
reporter's name from the prosaic Johnny

Jones to the more imposing Huntley Haverstock, to sound more like a foreign correspondent.

The scene shifts to Europe, where McCrea manages a brief interview with a highly respected diplomat (Albert Basserman) who is then assassinated as he is about to attend a peace conference. From then on, it's McCrea chasing and being chased by an assortment of sinister spies—including the usually benign Edmund Gwen, who tries to push McCrea off the top of a building but plunges to his own death instead. Tagging along with McCrea are Robert Benchley, as the inept foreign correspondent he was sent to assist, and George Sanders, as a suave English correspondent. On the way, McCrea meets and falls in love with Larraine Day, the daughter of Herbert Marshall, a "peace front" spokesman who turns out to be a Nazi agent.

After a plane carrying McCrea back to America is shot down and he and Miss Day are picked up by a rescue ship, McCrea manages to phone his story to the paper, in true newspaper movie style. "He wouldn't phone if it weren't a story," says editor Davenport with executive shrewdness — and orders the presses held.

It may all seem a little stale now, but at the time the movie was widely accepted, partly because Hitchcock's flair for making kidnappings, narrow escapes, and other such high adventures both grippingly vivid and wryly amusing was at its peak.

The movie's instant success—and the spread of the war—made the foreign correspondent a popular film hero, and the war years gave us many more movies about American newsmen involved in wartime intrigues. Most of them couldn't touch Hitchcock's pacesetter, but a few are worth mentioning.

There was, for example, *Confirm or Deny* (1941), with Don Ameche as a U.S. correspondent in London during the days of the blitz. Samuel Fuller had a hand in the story, which called for Ameche—by means too implausible to go into—to get hold of Hitler's invasion plans, and then suffering the newsman's most frustrating dilemma: to publish the story (a scoop!) would seriously jeopardize England's defense.

Confirm or Deny. To a foreign correspondent like Don Ameche, nobody's telephone is off limits. (20th Century-Fox, 1941)

(Now that the war was "real," you'll notice a difference between McCrea's behavior and Ameche's: McCrea's resourcefulness in *Foreign Correspondent* is admirable when he tells his big story to an unsuspecting sea captain while the New York editor eavesdrops via an open radio line; Ameche must rise above his professional creed and suppress his story rather than risk the defeat of our ally.)

Not every Hollywood producer had his finger on the public pulse. Leo McCarey apparently thought the Nazis still funny in 1942. He made a wartime comedy called *Once Upon a Honeymoon,* with Cary Grant and Ginger Rogers, that seems grotesquely ill-advised in retrospect.

Grant is an American reporter in Warsaw in the days when Hitler had just invaded that city. Miss Rogers is an American chorus girl married to a Nazi villain (Walter Slezak), and eventually she and Grant fall in love and he rescues her. Even forgetting the question of why she married the Nazi in the first place, one is left wondering what she would have done if Grant hadn't turned up.

(The subject of Nazis as comic villains was far more skillfully handled by Ernst Lubitsch in the vastly amusing *To Be or Not To Be*, with Jack Benny and Carole Lombard.)

The war in the Pacific was also covered by Hollywood-made foreign correspondents. An

Once Upon a Honeymoon. Correspondent Cary Grant saved Ginger Rogers from the Nazis in this flimsy comedy. (RKO, 1942)

example was *Somewhere I'll Find You* (1942), with Clark Gable and Lana Turner. Gable and Robert Sterling are brothers, both correspon-

Somewhere I'll Find You. Robert Sterling and Clark Gable were a brother team of foreign correspondents. (MGM, 1942)

dents, who are ordered home to New York by a publisher who disregards their warnings of an impending war. Gable has a brief romantic encounter with Miss Turner, then learns that she is engaged to his brother. Lana switches her allegiance to Gable, who now gives her the cold shoulder.

When the two brothers are finally sent to Indochina to cover the war, they find Lana there, slightly smudged but still glamorous, smuggling Chinese children to safety.

Eventually, brother Sterling is killed at Bataan, leaving Gable and Turner to justify the film's title. A routine mixture of romance, melodrama, and wartime propaganda, it was nevertheless the kind of yarn audiences of the time went for.

The adventures of war correspondents, some less likely than others, continued through the early 1940s. In 1942, Dana Andrews starred in a mundane film, playing the title role in *Berlin Correspondent.* The same year produced one of the sillier wartime comedies, *The Lady Has Plans,* with Paulette Goddard as a correspondent in Lisbon who is mistaken for a spy, and Ray Milland as an American radio correspondent who goes to her aid.

Even Bob Hope had a fling at playing a foreign correspondent—recalled to Washington in disgrace, then tangling with a nest of spies—in *They Got Me Covered* (1943), with Dorothy Lamour as his amour and Otto Preminger as a menacing Nazi.

The gift of omniscience was often conferred upon newsmen in movies, and particularly on foreign correspondents during wartime films. Thus, in *Blood on the Sun* (1945), we had James Cagney as a prewar correspondent in Tokyo, forseeing the threat to democracy, uncovering plans of aggression. And, of course, when no one will listen to him, Cagney has no choice but to plunge into the nest of villains and do them in almost alone.

Then there were those big, action-filled, heroic wartime films, some of them animated recruiting posters designed to stir us all up and cheer the boys at the front. Now and then, war correspondents were sprinkled among the "typical" American boys in these films. In *Guadalcanal Diary* (1943), which had Preston

Assignment, Paris. Dana Andrews (left) was a foreign correspondent, working with George Sanders. A decade earlier Andrews had a similar role in *Berlin Correspondent*. (Columbia, 1952)

The Lady Has Plans. Ray Milland (left) goes on the air to help Paulette Goddard in this wartime spy story. (Paramount, 1942)

They Got Me Covered. Bob Hope was a comic foreign correspondent hiding from Axis spies in Washington. (RKO, 1943)

Blood on the Sun. Veteran foreign correspondents meet. Wallace Ford (left) and James Cagney. (United Artists, 1945)

Foster, Lloyd Nolan, and William Bendix heading the cast, there was Reed Hadley as a war correspondent.

And Errol Flynn's famous wartime film, *Objective, Burma* (1945)—famous partly because it managed to offend the British, who felt their part in the Burma invasion had been glossed over—gave us a fairly human war correspondent, played by Henry Hull, who didn't quite complete the long march.

Probably the least pretentious and most deeply moving film made about a war correspondent was *The Story of G.I. Joe,* made in 1945 in tribute to Ernie Pyle, the least preten-

tious and most human of American reporters covering the Second World War. Ostensibly, the star was Robert Mitchum as a grimly realistic infantry captain. But it was Burgess Meredith's sensitive portrayal of Ernie Pyle, and the understated writing and direction, that made the film so affecting.

Humphrey Bogart was a heroic newsman in *Passage to Marseille* (1944), although that part of the story was more of a subplot. Bogart was a crusading Parisian editor who opposed France's appeasement of Hitler. He was promptly framed on a murder charge and carted off to Devil's Island. Much of the movie

Objective, Burma. Foreign correspondent Henry Hull
(center) is about to jump into war. Flanking him are
Errol Flynn and George Tyne. (Warner Brothers, 1945)

The Story of G.I. Joe. Burgess Meredith (center) played famed correspondent Ernie Pyle in this war film. At left is Robert Mitchum. (United Artists, 1945)

Passage to Marseilles. Humphrey Bogart and Michelle Morgan. He was an editor hounded out of print, then jailed by the Vichy government of France. (Warner Brothers, 1944)

deals with the attempts of Bogart and a ship-load of other escapees to seize the French freighter that has picked them up and get it to England.

There was more froth than substance to *Lover Come Back* (1946), which had George Brent as a war correspondent, Lucille Ball as his neglected wife, and Vera Zorina as a shapely photographer who spent far more time with Brent than Miss Ball could appreciate.

With the war over, there were now movies gifted with hindsight, and some of them dealt with the exploits of newsmen in wartime.

One such was *Malaya* (1949), with James Stewart as a veteran foreign correspondent who is tapped by the U.S. government during the Second World War to help smuggle rubber out of Malaya, right from under the noses of the Japanese. He teams up with an experienced smuggler (Spencer Tracy) and the two of them proceed to make the Japanese look like chumps. The fact that Stewart was supposed to be a newspaperman was almost incidental in this film, if not altogether irrelevant. By way of giving Stewart a little human trait, he was an incessant cigarette moocher in the movie. Whether that can be regarded as typical of reporters is a debatable point.

Clark Gable was back to playing foreign correspondent again (and also outwitting communists) in *Never Let Me Go*, made in 1953. This time, Gable is in Moscow at the war's end and falls in love with Russian bal-

Lover Come Back. George Brent was the roving correspondent, Lucille Ball his jealous wife, and Vera Zorina (center) the reason for her jealousy. (Universal, 1946)

Malaya. Spencer Tracy and James Stewart, hiding from a Japanese officer. Stewart was a foreign correspondent on a mission for the U.S. Government. (MGM, 1949)

Never Let Me Go. Foreign correspondent Clark Gable, in Moscow again, fell for a Russian ballerina, then plotted to get her out of Russia. (MGM, 1954)

lerina Gene Tierney. After he's deported, he makes plans for his wife to escape in a small ship he and a friend have bought for the purpose, but Miss Tierney is detained—she has to dance for a Russian general—so Gable swims ashore, poses as a Russian officer, and spirits his wife through the Iron Curtain.

The cycle of war-correspondent films was rapidly fizzling. In 1957, Larry Parks (hounded out of Hollywood by the mid-1950s witch hunters) turned up in an English-made movie playing an American correspondent in London who gets wind of a ring of international thieves and goes to work cleaning them out. The movie, titled *Tiger by the Tail,* was released in American theaters as *Cross-Up.**

Cross-Up. Larry Parks was an American reporter up to his phone in London crime. (United Artists, 1957)

But the romantic image of the American reporter in foreign lands still persisted. In 1958, Lana Turner played a lady foreign correspondent in wartime Britain in a movie titled *Another Time, Another Place.* Her leading men were Sean Connery and Barry Sullivan, and Miss Turner spent more time falling in and out of love than she did filing stories.

---

*This may be as good a place as any to refer to the omission of English films from this survey of newsmen. There have, of course, been English films about the press, including *This Man is News,* with Barry K. Barnes, *A Run for Your Money,* with Alec Guinness, and *Front Page Story,* with Jack Hawkins. But British cinema somehow never made the popular hero of the reporter that Hollywood did, so his appearances there have been far less frequent.

In 1959, Robert Mitchum played an American war correspondent in Greece at the time of the Nazi invasion of that country. The film was called *The Angry Hills* and the cast included Gia Scala and Stanley Baker.

Although it concerned itself with deeper matters, *Lawrence of Arabia* (1962) gave us a good portrayal of a foreign correspondent in a different era. This was the cynical, hardboiled Bentley, ably interpreted by Arthur Kennedy.

The 1972 film, *Young Winston,* with Simon Ward in the title role, dealt with the formative years of Winston Churchill's eventful life and the twisted relationship of his parents, played by Anne Bancroft and Robert Shaw. But it also included Churchill's celebrated stint as a foreign correspondent in the Boer War, during which he was captured and then effected a bold escape that helped make the young man famous.

In 1968, the Second World War was the backdrop for yet another foreign correspondent role for Robert Mitchum. The film was *Anzio,* one of those supposedly definitive movies about specific wartime events. The cast this time had Peter Falk, Arthur Kennedy, Robert Ryan, and other capable actors, but Mitchum's correspondent role was less impressive amid all the fighting.

David Janssen played a television journalist (the present-day equivalent of the old foreign correspondent) in *The Shoes of the Fisherman* (1968), but his role was both superfluous and senseless. The film was about a Russian (Anthony Quinn) who is named Pope of the Catholic Church. Apart from being involved in a wholly extraneous love story, Janssen's main purpose seemed to be to occasionally inform the audience as to the procedures by which a Pope is elected. The role is something of an offense to audiences, because the implication is that they are too simple-minded to understand what is going on without having it all explained to them. Worse than that, it is an offense to moviemaking, because it is such a clumsy way of tackling a basic problem of exposition.

As it happened, David Janssen was also involved in another film the same year that presented a strange portrait of a foreign cor-

Another Time, Another Place. Somewhat more glamorous than your average foreign correspondent was Lana Turner. (Paramount, 1958)

The Angry Hills. Robert Mitchum, correspondent in Greece during the Nazi invasion. (MGM, 1959)

Lawrence of Arabia. Correspondent Arthur Kennedy followed Peter O'Toole's adventures in this big film. (Columbia, 1962)

Young Winston. Simon Ward, as young Churchill, was a war correspondent Kent captured by the Boers, then escaped. (Columbia, 1972)

Anzio. Robert Mitchum was reporting the war again. At
right is Peter Falk. (Columbia, 1968)

The Shoes of the Fisherman. David Janssen (left) was a
television newsman covering the arrival of Pope-to-be
Anthony Quinn at Rome. (MGM, 1968)

The Green Berets. David Janssen in Vietnam as a correspondent learned which side John Wayne's views were buttered on. At left is Patrick Wayne. (Warner Brothers, 1968)

respondent. This was *The Green Berets* (1968), the John Wayne epic designed to justify American involvement in Vietnam. Janssen was simply a punching bag, a prop set up to be knocked down by superhawk Wayne's irrefutable saber-rattling.

Janssen played a "liberal" correspondent who accompanies the Green Berets to Vietnam "to see for myself." But even before he sees anything, he is being barraged by pro-intervention arguments. When he points out that South Vietnam has no constitution, Aldo Ray, one of Wayne's stauncher supporters in the film, tells Janssen:

"The thirteen colonies had no constitution

... What's involved here is communist domination of the world."

At another point, Wayne lectures Janssen: "Out here (in Vietnam) due process is a bullet."

Much of the dialogue sounds like Pentagon slogans, and Wayne's frontier philosophy keeps shining through. "It's hard to talk to anybody about this country who hasn't seen it," he says.

Eventually, Janssen has his eyes opened by Viet Cong atrocities (all this, of course, was about a year before the My Lai story broke) and he's ripe for recruiting when a soldier puts the question to him: "That's what it's all about. . . . You gonna stand there and referee or you gonna help us?'' Janssen opts to help "us.''

It was probably inevitable that the least popular war in America's history should also have resulted in a movie in which the role of the foreign correspondent is so distorted by the hysteria of the jingoist minority who persisted in supporting that war right down to the day when Mr. Nixon invented that remarkable bit of myopic euphemism called ''peace with honor.''

6

THE REPORTER AS HUMAN BEING

One of the reasons for the success of *The Front Page,* first on stage and then on screen, was that Hecht and MacArthur created believable, living, breathing central characters — not perfect heroes and unmitigated villains, but imperfect human beings with conflicting emotions and goals.

However obvious it may seem that this is simply a basic necessity in creating any sort of fictional character, the startling thing is how often it is ignored. In the years following *The Front Page,* the newspaperman became something of a robot—mechanically mouthing the accepted clichés of the newspaper movie, mindlessly insulting the editor, illogically solving crimes.

In those days of burgeoning box-office receipts, "product" was needed to keep the theaters filled, "programmers" to fill the bottom half of double bills, "quickies" to enable exhibitors to change programs two or three times a week, to keep the customers coming back again and again. As was to be said, much later, of television, the studios' slogan seemed to be: "We don't want it great, we want it Tuesday."

As with any other kind of movie, the newspaper films that linger longest in the memory are often those in which director and writer — and actors, too — had the wit to remember that they were presenting people who had to behave more or less in a way audiences would find it possible to believe.

In some cases, movie makers even managed to invent stories in which the characters were human beings first and newspaper reporters second. At such times, we, the audience, were treated to the joy of discovering that newspaper people, like anyone else, could have problems, wives, children, debts, homes, hobbies, crises, idiosyncrasies, habits, relationships, pleasures, and sorrows—not always connected with their work.

Not surprisingly, one director who understood the need for depicting reasonably rounded characters was Frank Capra, whose *It Happened One Night* was a landmark in the development of romantic comedies with newspaper backgrounds.

But *It Happened One Night* was not Capra's first effort in the genre. In 1931, aware of the success of *The Front Page,* Capra elected to do a comedy with a newspaper setting. Called *Platinum Blonde,* it had Robert Williams and Loretta Young as chummy reporters, plus Jean Harlow as the platinum blonde who comes between them. They proved an amusing triangle, with Williams being lured by the society girl (Harlow) but eventually returning to his newsroom pal, Loretta.

If nothing else, this little comedy served as a warm-up for Capra's forthcoming smash hit with Gable and Colbert. In subsequent films, Capra was to give us a whole gallery of interesting (often human) newspaper people — Jean Arthur in *Mr. Deeds Goes to Town;* Thomas Mitchell in *Mr. Smith Goes to Washington;* Barbara Stanwyck and Edward Arnold in *Meet John Doe;* and several others to be covered elsewhere in this survey.

Phil Stong, a newspaperman turned

117

Platinum Blonde. Robert Williams, reporter, is torn between Loretta Young and Jean Harlow. (Columbia, 1931)

novelist, was responsible for a book that Hollywood got pretty fair mileage out of. One of the central characters in it was a likable newspaper reporter.

The story was *State Fair,* first filmed in 1933 with Will Rogers, Janet Gaynor, and Lew Ayres in the leads. Rogers was Abel Frake, head of the Iowa family that heads to the state fair full of dreams and hopes. Miss Gaynor was Margie, the shy young daughter who is swept off her feet by Pat Gilbert (Ayres), the dashing young reporter she meets at the fair. Frank's son (played by Norman Foster) also has a romantic encounter at the fair, but with less enduring results.

For Ayres, it was only the second in a string of newspaper roles he was to play (*Okay, America* was made a year earlier), but it was different from most of the others in that it concerned more the personal side of a newsman's life, rather than his headline hunting.

State Fair was remade in 1945, with Jeanne Crain as the young girl and Dana Andrews as the newspaperman she falls in love with. This version was notable chiefly for the musical score provided by Rodgers and Hammerstein, then at the peak of their form.

A third, and considerably less satisfying, version of *State Fair* was made in 1962, with

State Fair. Janet Gaynor and Lew Ayres played the romantic leads in this film. Ayres was a newspaperman. (Fox, 1933)

State Fair. The next time around, Dana Andrews and Jeanne Crain played the same roles. (20th Century-Fox, 1945)

Pat Boone, Ann-Margret, Bobby Darin, Tom Ewell, and Alice Faye heading the cast. It bore little resemblance to the original.

James Stewart had a sympathetic role as a newspaper reporter in *The Last Gangster* (1937), in which his problem was more human than work-related. Edward G. Robinson had the title role, a gangster trying to outlive his passing era. Robinson's wife (Rose Stradner) is innocent of his underworld activities, but when Stewart writes stories defending her, he is fired. When Robinson goes to jail, the wife, now carrying his child, divorces him and marries Stewart. Some years later, Robinson emerges, determined to find his wife and son. Eventually, all the bad guys kill each other off, and Stewart is left in peace with his wife and adopted son.

The Man Who Came to Dinner. Vamp Ann Sheridan tried to lure reporter Richard Travis in this bright comedy. (Warner Brothers, 1942)

The Last Gangster. Edward G. Robinson played the title role, Rose Stradner and Douglas Scott were his wife and son, and that's James Stewart behind the mustache, an upstanding young reporter who wound up with Robinson's family. (MGM, 1937)

In 1939, George S. Kaufman, one of the American theater's wittiest writers (and, incidentally, a formidable newspaperman in his earlier days) wrote *The Man Who Came to Dinner,* in collaboration with Moss Hart.

This smash hit play was based quite broadly on the life-style of the colorful Alexander Woolcott, one of the best known columnist-critic-personalities of the time. (For the play,

Woolcott was called Sheridan Whiteside, and Monty Woolley played him on both stage and screen. But both Kaufman and Woolcott played Whiteside on the stage for short periods.)

The irascible Whiteside, one of the most delightfully detestable characters in modern American dramatic literature, combined the flamboyant ego of subject Woolcott and the devastating wit of author Kaufman.

But there was a secondary newspaper character in *The Man Who Came to Dinner.* He was Bert Jefferson, reporter and editor of the *Mesalia Journal,* in the small Ohio town where Whiteside is stranded with a broken leg. In the 1942 film version, Jefferson was played by Richard Travis.

Jefferson comes to interview Whiteside and promptly falls in love with Maggie Cutler (Bette Davis), Whiteside's invaluable secretary. To rupture the romance and avoid losing his secretary, Whiteside throws Jefferson into the clutches of Lorraine Sheldon, a Hollywood siren (played on the screen by Ann Sheridan). But in the end, Maggie outmaneuvers both Lorraine and Whiteside and runs off with her young newspaperman.

In 1941, producer Joseph L. Mankiewicz and screen writer Ring Lardner, Jr. (both onetime newspapermen) were involved in *Woman of the Year,* one of the happiest of the

Woman of the Year. Spencer Tracy and Katharine Hepburn both played newspaper types. Yes, that's Roscoe Karns at right. (MGM, 1941)

Spencer Tracy-Katharine Hepburn collaborations.

Tracy was a New York sports columnist and Miss Hepburn was a world-affairs pundit for the same paper. Their early feud blossoms into romance and they marry, only to discover that their busy, sometimes conflicting careers interfere with any chance of a happy marriage. In this pre-Women's Lib time, obviously, the woman turns out to be in the wrong and ends up submitting to her husband's will. Nevertheless, *Woman of the Year* was fully entertaining and proved a big box-office success.

A similar exercise in husband-wife conflict, with a press background, was *Designing Woman,* made in 1957, with Gregory Peck and

Designing Woman. Mickey Shaughnessy was bodyguard to bold sportswriter Gregory Peck. (MGM, 1957)

Lauren Bacall. Although it didn't have quite the bite of *Woman of the Year*, it was an enjoyable comedy.

This time around, Peck was again a sports writer but his new bride, Miss Bacall, was a fashion designer. Their sharply contrasted backgrounds made for even greater conflict and, to add some spice, the script tossed in a touch of jealousy: Dolores Gray, an old flame of Peck's keeps turning up. The film's best moments came when Peck, hiding out from sports-world mobsters, holed up in a New York hotel with dim-witted bodyguard Mickey Shaughnessy, while wife Bacall thought he was out of town.

Sometimes the main story could dominate the proceedings to the extent that the newspaper connection became lost in the shuffle. In *Penny Serenade* (1941), Cary Grant was a gadabout reporter who met and fell in love with Irene Dunne. Assigned to Japan, he took her with him, then promptly quit his job there (because he'd inherited some small amount of money) and returned to the States, where they bought a dying smalltown newspaper. While in Japan, they survived an earthquake, but the child she was carrying didn't, and she couldn't have any more. So they decided to adopt one, but had a tough time qualifying because of their financial insecurity: the newly acquired

Guest Wife. Claudette Colbert posed as correspondent Don Ameche's wife in this comedy. (United Artists, 1945)

little newspaper wasn't doing well. An emotional appeal by Grant melted the heart of a stern judge and they were allowed to keep their adopted daughter. But the child soon died, and the Grant-Dunne marriage seemed doomed—until the kindly lady at the orphanage (Beulah Bondi) found another child for them to adopt. As for the newspaper, it was never again mentioned after about the middle of the movie. Still, this was an effective tearjerker, well directed by George Stevens, and engagingly acted by the principals.

Far less satisfying was a 1945 comedy concerning some contrived problems of a war correspondent (Don Ameche) and the lady who agrees to pose as his wife (Claudette Colbert). The movie was titled *Guest Wife* and it did little to enhance the reputations of its two stars.

Decidedly more acceptable was *June Bride*, with Bette Davis and Robert Montgomery, made in 1948. This time, as in *Woman of the Year*, two journalists are thrown into conflict. Miss Davis played the editor of a slick woman's magazine, Montgomery was a foreign correspondent fresh out of wars to report. The publisher who employed both of them (Jerome Cowan) decided to make Montgomery assistant to Miss Davis, a decision frought with Hollywood possibilities.

Penny Serenade. Edgar Buchanan played the folksy typesetter, and Gary Grant and Irene Dunne were the city types who took over the shaky small-town paper. (Columbia, 1941)

June Bride. Bette Davis was the boss lady (editor) and Robert Montgomery her resentful employee. (Warner Brothers, 1948)

Their first assignment together is to cover a June wedding (in the dead of winter, because magazines plan months ahead) in a small Indiana town. Somewhat in the manner of

On Our Merry Way. Burgess Meredith did man-on-the-street interviews in this all-star flop. (United Artists, 1948)

Sheridan Whiteside, Montgomery proceeds to upset the lives of the small town family. Although his meddling ruins Miss Davis's planned cover story, he does help straighten out the romantic entanglements of the young people involved. In the end, Bette—still adhering to the current ethic that a woman's place is in the home—tosses her career away to marry Montgomery. Despite its traditional approach to the battle of the sexes, *June Bride* was a sprightly comedy and once more showed us the human side of life among journalists.

The same year saw an admirable, though unsuccessful, attempt at showing the reporter at work—without crime, violence, or scandal involved. The movie was titled *On Our Merry Way* (1948) and was co-produced by Burgess Meredith, who also played the reporter.

Actually Meredith was a classified ad clerk on a Los Angeles newspaper, yearning to be a reporter. His wife (Paulette Goddard) prodded him into posing as his paper's man-in-the-street reporter to dig up some human interest stories. From there on, however, Meredith became merely a link between the stories he came across. The characters he encountered were played by James Stewart, Henry Fonda, Dorothy Lamour, Victor Moore, Fred MacMurray, William Demarest, and Hugh Herbert. But even with all that box-office bait, the picture flopped. (As one Hollywood sage long ago observed, "an all-star cast is a no-star cast.")

The prolific Frank Capra came up with yet another newspaperman-as-human-being story in 1951. This was *Here Comes the Groom*, with Bing Crosby and Jane Wyman. Bing played a happy-go-lucky roving reporter who became attached to three French orphans and decided to adopt them, only to learn he wouldn't be allowed to do so because he had no wife. He promply nominated Miss Wyman to fill the bill, then discovered he had to woo her away from rival Franchot Tone. Besides the deft direction of Capra, the film had an added blessing: any time the plot drooped, Crosby could (and did) toss in a song.

Crosby was a journalist again two years later in *Little Boy Lost* (1953), without benefit of Capra's direction, but with a perfectly capable George Seaton at the helm. This was a

Here Comes the Groom. Bing Crosby, a foreign correspondent, had Franchot Tone (left) as his rival. The man wearing glasses is Walter Catlett, a veteran movie reporter. (Paramount, 1951)

Little Boy Lost. Again a correspondent, seeking a son born in wartime, was Bing Crosby. (Paramount, 1953)

rather more serious film, in which Crosby was a Second World War correspondent who returned to France in search of an illegitimate son he'd never seen. Crosby had already proven his ability as a straight actor, and this movie added yet another sensitive portrayal to his credits.

At the other extreme was *Carnival Story* (1954), a rather grubby melodrama with Anne Baxter, Steve Cochran, and George Nader. Miss Baxter played a carnival aerialist whose partner is killed by barker Cochran. Nader was a magazine writer-photographer who got involved in the sawdust intrigue. In time, Nader was marked as Cochran's next target, but things weren't allowed to proceed that far—only far enough to be a total bore.

The human side of a sports writer's life was absorbingly depicted in *The Harder They Fall*, which was Humphrey Bogart's last movie, made in 1956.

Bogart played an ex-sports writer who is hired by fight promoter Rod Steiger to publicize a great Argentine giant of a fighter, played by Mike Lane. When the pathetic Lane survives a brutal fight and tries to collect the money he believes is coming to him, Steiger coldly tells the fighter he has only fifty dollars coming to him. Disgusted by the inhumanity of the fight racket, Bogart gives Lane his own share of the proceeds and then vows to write a series of articles exposing the hoodlums who control boxing.

With a taut script adapted from Budd Schulberg's hard-boiled novel, *The Harder They Fall* was an impressive film, stripping the

Carnival Story. That's Anne Baxter being rescued from the tank. The rest of the picture remained unrescued. (RKO, 1954)

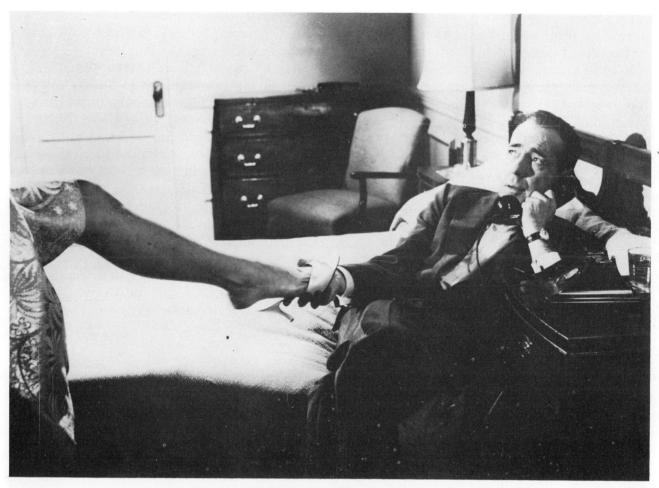

The Harder They Fall. Humphrey Bogart was the seasoned sportswriter turned boxing publicist. The leg may belong to Jan Sterling. (Columbia, 1956)

glamour off the prize-ring world and providing Bogart with just the kind of role at which he was unbeatable.

But *The Harder They Fall* was an exception to the rule. Usually, Hollywood's grasp of the workings of a newspaper's sports department was naively limited. In 1950, for example, Dick Powell played a fairly unlikely sports writer in *Right Cross,* a mish-mash of a melodrama about the prize ring. Ricardo Montalban was the embittered Mexican-American prize fighter, and June Allyson was the girl who loved him.

Powell's sports columnist was such a big wheel that when Montalban injured his hand while sparring, almost his first concern was that Powell "get the story." (This was incom-

Right Cross. Ricardo Montalban nurses a shiner while sportswriter Dick Powell and trainer John Gallaudet look on. (MGM, 1950)

prehensible in that throughout the rest of the film Montalban kept trying to hide the seriousness of the injury.) But Dick, it soon developed, was otherwise occupied: he was tying one on because he, too, was in love with June Allyson.

After all the standard fight movie clichés, there's a fairly lively fight, which Montalban loses. He then further injures his fist on Powell's jaw, but he wins June.

In a way, *Right Cross* is a good example of the dangers of relegating the newspaperman to something approximating his real-life role of observer and reporter: the main story gets away from him, and *Right Cross* becomes much more Montalban's film.

The trials and tribulations of those journalists who work as critics have been touched on now and then in films. One example was *Critic's Choice* (1963), with Bob Hope as the critic faced with the problem of deciding whether or not ethics permitted him to review his wife's play. The wife was Lucille Ball, and this teaming of two skilled comedy players yielded enough laughs to make the exercise worthwhile.

Not quite as acceptable was *Please Don't Eat the Daisies,* with Doris Day and David Niven, in 1963. This was based on the funny book by Jean Kerr, wife of New York theater critic Walter Kerr. (They, supposedly, were the models for *Critic's Choice*.) But it dealt more with the home life of a theater critic (Niven), complicated by the busy-busy activities of his wife and children.

No critic ever had a wilder time than the one

Critic's Choice. That's Bob Hope gazing away from his empty typewriter. With him are Ricky Kelman and Jessie Royce Landis. (Warner Brothers, 1963)

127

Please Dont' Eat the Daisies. David Niven explains the facts of criticism to Doris Day. (MGM, 1963)

played by Cary Grant in *Arsenic and Old Lace* (1944), the Frank Capra version of the hit Broadway play. Grant was the theater critic who discovered that his two aunts (Josephine Hull and Jean Adair) have been murdering lonely old men and burying them in the cellar of their Brooklyn house. Things got even more out of hand when Grant's brother Jonathan and his creepy aid turned up. They were far madder killers than the two delightful aunts. (One of the play's jokes was in having Boris Karloff, as Jonathan, complaining that "Dr. Einstein," his flunkey, had made him look like Boris Karloff. But this was lost in the film, because Capra cast Raymond Massey instead of Karloff in the Jonathan part.)

Arsenic and Old Lace. Tied up critic Cary Grant is at the mercy of Raymond Massey and Peter Lorre, while policeman Jack Carson ponders helping him. (Warner Brothers, 1944)

Even though the movie wasn't quite the smash hit the play had been, Grant and the others—and particularly the Misses Hull and Adair—made it a funny romp.

The newspaperman in love has, of course, sparked any number of movies, ranging from very good to intolerable. Among the more serious was *Love Is a Many Splendored Thing* (1955), in which William Holden was a foreign correspondent in Hong Kong who fell in love with Eurasian doctor Jennifer Jones. The Korean War was only one of the matters interfering with their romance. Other complications involved the racial difference between them, plus the fact that Holden was already married. A kind of modern *Madame Butterfly*,* the film was unrelievedly romantic, but the skilled performances helped keep the plot afloat.

A New Kind of Love. Joanne Woodward and Paul Newman starred in this dreary comedy. (Paramount, 1963)

Love Is a Many Splendored Thing. The Korean War was only one of the problems faced by Jennifer Jones and William Holden. (20th Century-Fox, 1955)

Different, and less rewarding, was *A New Kind of Love* (1963), with Paul Newman and Joanne Woodward. This awkward comedy had Newman as a jaded columnist on a two-week vacation in Paris, looking for a "new angle." (He never did explain to what he was seeking a new angle, just a new angle.) He

meets and pursues fashion-world executive Woodward through an interminable series of cute Parisian escapades, most of which are not worth relating. The whole movie marked one of the lowest points in the Newman-Woodward careers.

More amusing was *Quick Before It Melts* (1964), with George Maharis and Robert Morse as two New York newsmen sent to Antarctica to study the manners and mores of the frozen south. The two men eventually

Quick, Before It Melts. Robert Morse and Anjanette Comer, with an uninvited snoop, find love in subzero weather. (MGM, 1965)

*Even the film's title song echoed melodically the aria, "Un bel di" from the Puccini opera.

manage to cause an international incident that falls rather shy of being hilarious, but the movie has its entertaining moments.

One of the funniest of human beings peripherally connected with newspaper work was Oscar Madison, the creation of Neil Simon in his Broadway play, *The Odd Couple*. Oscar, America's most celebrated slob, was a New York sports writer, recently divorced, who teamed up with Felix Unger, a photographer whose marriage had also broken up. When the play was transferred to the screen, Walter Matthau was Oscar and Jack Lemmon played Felix. Both they and the script were hilarious and *The Odd Couple* eventually gave birth to a television series (with Jack Klugman and Tony Randall) that soon became a weekly favorite.

Back in 1941, that unforgettable film, *Citizen Kane,* gave us a couple of studies of newspapermen as human beings. The title character of Charles Foster Kane will be discussed in a subsequent chapter, but the other one bears mention here.

He was Jed Leland, the character that served to introduce Joseph Cotten to the screen. Jed was one of Kane's loyal followers, idolizing his wealthy benefactor (Kane made him a drama critic) until he gradually learned that the high ideals expressed by Kane were not to be taken too seriously.

When Leland and Kane have a falling out, Leland asks to be transferred from New York to Chicago, where Kane owns another paper. They don't see each other for some time, until Kane's second wife, Susan Alexander, is to

The Odd Couple. As Jack Lemmon eats, sportswriter Walter Matthau sprays a fly in this Neil Simon comedy. (Paramount, 1968)

Citizen Kane. Joseph Cotten and Everett Sloane look
on while publisher Orson Welles sets down his creed.
(RKO, 1941)

Citizen Kane. Reporter William Alland and major domo
Paul Stewart survey some of the art treasure collected
by Kane. At left, over Alland's shoulder, is Alan Ladd.
(RKO, 1941)

make her operatic debut in Chicago—and Leland must write the review. The lady happens to be a talentless singer whose career has been stubbornly pushed by the egocentric Kane.

Jed Leland served as Kane's conscience and, one tends to suspect, as the voice of Herman Mankiewicz, the ex-newsman turned screen writer who worked with Orson Welles on the screenplay of *Citizen Kane*. Both critic Pauline Kael and John Houseman, an associate of Welles's for many years, give much of the credit for the Kane script to Mankiewicz, even though the screen credit is shared by the two men.

But no matter who invented them, the newspaper people in *Citizen Kane* are among the most human, least artificial of any ever delineated in films. Nor did Mankiewicz's interest in newsmen end with the flamboyant Kane and the disillusioned Leland. The film also gives us a glimpse of a serious, hard-working, unglamorous newsman at work. This is Thompson (played by William Alland), the reporter assigned to dig into the life of the deceased Charles Foster Kane. (As a kind of bonus, movie buffs can also spot Alan Ladd, in a bit part as another reporter.)

Sharply contrasted from the slanted realism attempted in *Citizen Kane* is the whimsey of a 1944 film by Rene Clair, titled *It Happened Tomorrow*. The script was by Dudley Nichols,

former reporter and foreign correspondent, and in a way it represented the ultimate daydream of any reporter. Larry Stevens (played by Dick Powell) is a newspaperman in the 1890s who meets a strange little man (George Cleveland) who has the knack of giving Powell a scoop on tomorrow's news, before it happens. Cub reporter Powell capitalizes on this by grabbing desirable bylines on big stories that nobody else has. The wry twist comes when, after several glorious days of this, Powell is given a scoop he didn't bargain for: his own obituary. Unusual though this fantasy was, it went the way of most Hollywood movies of the time—insistently reaching for an implausible but happy ending.

One aspect of the Second World War brought forth a touching drama that moved millions of fans to tears and also introduced a moppet named Margaret O'Brien to film audiences. Titled *Journey for Margaret* (1942) it dealt with the tragedy of children orphaned by

It Happened Tomorrow. George Cleveland, Dick Powell, Edgar Kennedy, and Linda Darnell. Reporter Powell had an edge on his rivals. (United Artists, 1944)

Journey for Margaret. Larraine Day and correspondent Robert Young comfort Billy Severn and Margaret O'Brien during an air attack on London. (MGM, 1942)

war. Robert Young played a war correspondent and Larraine Day was his pregnant wife, both fleeing France for London. There, the wife loses her unborn child, but Young becomes aware of the plight of many living orphans. The couple eventually take two of them (Margaret O'Brien and Billy Severn) to America with them. With no more plot than that, this sensitively made movie worked by making the seldom-realized horrors of war all too vivid.

Ernest Hemingway, perhaps the most celebrated of all former newspapermen, provided the original source material for the 1957 film, *The Sun Also Rises,* a story about the "lost generation" of which Hemingway had become the chief chronicler. In the Darryl F. Zanuck production based on the novel, Tyrone Power played Jake Barnes, the American newspaper correspondent whose First World War injury had left him impotent. That was a grave enough problem, but to be impotent and loved by Ava Gardner would seem insufferable.

However, 1957 was apparently not the time for a nostalgic movie about the 1920s. Or, perhaps transferring Hemingway to the screen is always a delicate matter. In any case, the film was not a major success, despite a competent performance by Power and a more impressive one by Errol Flynn as the boozy, cynical Mike Campbell.

The Sun Also Rises. Ava Gardner and Tyrone Power were among the stars in this Hemingway-based film. (20th Century-Fox, 1957)

Paris Interlude. Otto Kruger (center) was the embittered, one-armed correspondent. At left, Robert Young. (MGM, 1934)

A less pretentious and more superficial look at the "lost generation" was MGM's *Paris Interlude* (1934), in which Robert Young was a post-World War barfly in Paris, idolizing Otto Kruger, as a one-armed news correspondent. Kruger turned out to be rather less than perfect—as did the whole movie.

More impressive, despite its irritating flaws, was a 1959 attempt to show the torment of a newspaperman who succumbs to the anguish of people he's supposed to be writing about objectively. Back in 1932, Lee Tracy had starred in a movie called *Advice to the Lovelorn,* which, according to the credits, was "inspired by" Nathanael West's story, "Miss Lonelyhearts." It was nothing more than an ordinary melodrama. But twenty-seven years

later, Dore Schary made a more serious effort to capture the essence of West's disturbing yarn.

The film was titled *Lonelyhearts* and had Montgomery Clift in the role of the idealistic young reporter assigned to give advice to his newspaper's lovelorn readers. Unable to ignore the pathetic cries for help of the unhappy people who write to him, he permits himself to become involved with one of them. This is Maureen Stapleton, a love-starved housewife who invents a web of lies to lure Clift to her apartment because her loneliness demands it. Not all of the movie worked, but the part devoted to this shattering encounter remains strongly etched in the memory.

With the exception of romantic love—the

Lonelyhearts. Maureen Stapleton and Montgomery Clift in one of this film's more poignant moments. (United Artists, 1949)

wheat of movie plots—no other human problem seems to have afflicted movie newspapermen more often than drinking.

It is, sad to say, one of the indestructible clichés of American belief that all newspapermen keep a bottle of booze in the bottom drawer of their desks, that the corner saloon claims more of their time than the newsroom, that tippling among reporters is as inevitable as gambling is among Las Vegas tourists. This is neither more nor less logical than a dozen other prejudices many people cling to and which some Hollywood films have helped to perpetuate: all Scotsmen are tight-fisted; all farmers are religious; all blacks are oversexed; all bankers are crooked; all labor organizers are communists; all politicians are corrupt; all painters are demented; all newspapermen are lushes.

No one who has spent any time in the newspaper world would seriously claim that drinking is unknown there. Nor would it be accurate to suggest that there have not been some pretty heavy drinkers working on various newspapers. But the incidence of alcoholism is probably no higher in that profession than in a good many others.

Nevertheless, drinking and its attendant human problems can be the basis for good drama, and it is understandable that Hollywood has many times made use of this fact. And, once again, all those former newsmen who turned screen writers must share part of the blame for the overemphasis on drink as a big part of the reporter's life in films.

There have been many newspaper movies in which a certain amount of drinking took place, often in comedy situations. The newspaper "wake" in *Deadline, U.S.A.* is one example. Paul Muni's brief bender in *Hi, Nellie* is another. And, of course, the barroom scenes in *Park Row* were keyed to the plot.

To cite just a couple of more random examples, there was Richard Dix as a hard-drinking newsman in *No Marriage Ties* (1933), and Melvyn Douglas as a reporter-lush in *The Guilt of Janet Ames* (1947).

But on occasion, Hollywood films have taken a closer, more serious look at "problem" drinking, and a few of these have centered on press people.

An early instance of the tippling newsman in film was the 1932 drama titled *Merrily We Go to Hell,* starring Fredric March and Sylvia Sidney. Miss Sidney, noted in her day for suffering not so much in silence as in bursts of emotional sobs, had a rough time in this one. She was swept off her feet by reporter March, a talented fellow who couldn't quite stay off the sauce.

March got thoroughly tanked at their engagement party and even at the opening of his play (journalism was merely a stepping stone to greater things); and at their posh wedding he managed to lose the ring, so he produced a bottle opener and slipped this on Sylvia's finger.

His excessive drinking and also his carrying on with an old flame (after marriage, mind you) proved too much even for patient Sylvia, and they parted. It took her serious illness to bring him to his senses and a bedside reconciliation.

In 1938, Errol Flynn and Bette Davis, in that

Merrily We Go to Hell. For the wedding of Fredric March and Sylvia Sidney, Skeets Gallagher was best man. Both men were reporters. (Paramount, 1932)

order of billing, were starred in a Warner Brothers drama titled *The Sisters*. Bette was the eldest sister of the title. The other two, Anita Louise and Jane Bryan, had their own marital scuffles, but the film concentrated mostly on Bette's rough life with (and sometimes without) Flynn. He played a moderately capable newspaperman who had two imperfections: an itch to travel and a liking for the bottle.

Of course, they get married, and, of course, he deserts her, and, of course, she has a tough time of it. Later, there's a kindly employer (Ian Hunter, a career kindly employer) who wants to marry her, but errant Errol turns up again, posing a final dilemma for Bette.

Warners shot the ending two ways. In one ending, Bette chooses security and Hunter; in the other, her heart rules and she takes Flynn back. After sneak-previewing the picture both ways to test audience preference, the romantic, or Davis-Flynn, ending was the one released. Audiences, it seems, were no more hooked on realism than were studio bosses.

James Cagney gave us a portrait of a boozing newsman in *Come Fill the Cup* (1951), but this one had a few switches. Cagney pulled himself together and became that most substantial of all substantial citizens, the reformed alcoholic. Then, his publisher (Raymond Massey) "assigned" Cagney to help straighten up Gig Young, the publisher's nephew, who had now taken to heavy drinking.

To make things more difficult for Cagney, Young was married to Cagney's former

The Sisters. Bette Davis watches Errol Flynn in one of his more sober moments in this drama. (Warner Brothers, 1938)

Come Fill the Cup. Reporter James Cagney was a reformed alcoholic doing missionary work among the drinkers. (Warner Brothers, 1951)

sweetheart (Phyllis Thaxter) and as if that weren't enough there was a sprinkling of underworld activity to keep things from getting dull. Mainly, though, it was Cagney's strong performance that carried the movie.

In 1964, there was a fine though not widely heralded film called *The Luck of Ginger Coffey* that gave audiences yet another portrait of a newspaperman with problems. Ginger Coffey (superbly played by Robert Shaw) was a hopeless failure at everything, and his heavy drinking represented more a symptom of his insecurity than a cause of his troubles. But the Brian Moore script, from his own novel, made the newspaper office look sharply real, and among the supporting characters were some

The Luck of Ginger Coffey. Powys Thomas swings his cane wildly in the direction of luckless Robert Shaw. (Walter Reade-Sterling, Inc., 1964)

She Gets Her Man. Veteran drunk Jack Norton played a reporter. At left is Hugh O'Connell. (Universal, 1935)

convincing types played by Tom Harvey and Powys Thomas, the latter playing a rowdy newspaper drunkard.

Finally, this gallery of elbow-bending newsmen must include a toast to the late Jack Norton, who spent most of his Hollywood career playing drunks. Norton, who was, in fact, a nondrinker, could imitate a drunk so beautifully that he was in constant demand to do just that—and, it seemed, only that—in movie after movie for more than two decades.

Predictably, Norton managed a kind of double play: in 1935, in a Zasu Pitts comedy called *She Gets Her Man,* he was cast as a drunken newspaperman.

7
THE SOB SISTER

Long before Women's Liberation became anything resembling a popular cause, women were working on newspapers, both in real life and in newspaper movies.

Generally, it's true that the women on newspapers in the movies did more glamorous work than most of those who toiled on real papers. Too often, young female reporters, even on big city papers, have been confined to covering "social" news, "women's page" features, and the like. There have been notable exceptions, like Dorothy Thompson, Anne O'Hare McCormick, Marguerite Higgins, and Flora Lewis. But for every widely know female reporter who gets to cover top stories there have undoubtedly been thousands who spent most of their working lives at weddings, social events, interviewing outstanding mothers, listening to luncheon-club lecturers, or otherwise helping to fill those pages that editors know their female readers turn to habitually.

Today, women have made inroads into a number of hitherto exclusively male fields—in sports, certainly, in politics, even on some fire and police departments. But for many years, women working on newspapers had to fight the usual problem: an unshakable belief on the part of most editors that there were some jobs women just couldn't "handle" as well as men.

Nevertheless, there were times when a woman reporter could come in handy on big stories. More often than not these were crime stories, and women were frequently assigned to cover the human or color angles. If somebody accused of a crime happened to be a woman, a female reporter might be assigned to play up the emotional aspects of the story. Or, if the accused was a man, he might have a wife, girl friend or mother, and the woman reporter would be sent to interview such interested parties, again playing up the heart-tugging angles. What they wrote came to be referred to as *sob stories* and, indubitably, the sister reporter doing such work came to be known as a sob sister.*

Film writers and producers, familiar with the ways of newspapers, came early to the realization that there was grist here for the movie mills. Not only was the perennial battle of the sexes provided with an acceptable arena—the underrated girl reporter challenged to prove she's as capable as the male, the latter confident that no girl could possibly keep pace with him—but it also gave filmmakers the chance to provide meaty roles for their actresses, who might otherwise be relatively useless in newspaper films.

As far back as 1929—the first full year of talking pictures—actress Lola Lane was seen as a sob sister in a movie called *Speakeasy* in which her leading man (playing a reporter) was Stuart Erwin.

The same year, Carole Lombard and Robert Armstrong were teamed in *Big News*, playing husband and wife who are also reporters on rival newspapers. Armstrong's drinking al-

*In my 18 years on newspapers, I knew many female reporters but never heard one of them referred to as a sob sister. Slang dictionaries date the term to about 1925, but give no indication if it originated in newspapers or movies about newspapers.

most costs him his job, and as a further annoyance he is framed on a murder charge. Sob sister Carole comes charging to the rescue, successfully proving his innocence. (By the way, Lew Ayres, who was later to become a fairly busy movie reporter, played a copy boy in this one.)

In 1930, Claudette Colbert was a gossip columnist in *Young Man of Manhattan,* with Norman Foster, the love interest, playing a sports writer.

And in 1931, in a melodrama called *The Finger Points,* Richard Barthelmess was the reporter involved with some underworld figures, and Fay Wray was the helpful sob sister.

By now the term *sob sister* was considered sufficiently well-known that it was used as the title of a movie, in 1931, with Linda Watkins in the title part and James Dunn as both the hero and the spokesman for all those male chauvinist reporters who didn't believe she could "take it." Actually, Linda really hated the toughness of the newspaper world, but she came through bravely in the clutch.

The year 1931 also brought us a mixture of soap and violence called *Dance, Fools, Dance,* in which Joan Crawford starred as a sob sister. Actually, Joan was a socialite who had to go to work after Daddy lost everything in the stock market crash. To further burden Joan's broad shoulders, she had a no-good brother who got himself mixed up with some very unsavory underworld types headed by Clark Gable.

The paper where Joan worked assigned its star reporter (Cliff Edwards) to the story, but

Sob Sister. That's Linda Watkins on the phone, with James Dunn next to her. (Fox, 1931)

140

Dance, Fools, Dance. Sob sister Joan Crawford is rarin' to go. At right is Cliff Edwards. (MGM, 1931)

The Hell Cat. Minna Gombel and Benny Baker get the latest from reporter Robert Armstrong. Publicity release of the time described Baker as Armstrong's "Cameraman stooge." (Columbia, 1934)

he was promptly bumped off, so Joan was given the thorny task of gaining the confidence of Gable in order to get the goods on him. (Somehow, it all sounds like a George O'Brien western, but that's the way it went.) Joan succeeds, as we all knew she would, and thereby gains both the respect of her colleagues and marriage to the young millionaire (Lester Vail), who had heretofore considered her immature and flighty.

For some reason best known to Hollywoods's decision makers, half the sob sisters in movies started out as giddy heiresses who, when confronted with deadlines, headlines, and bylines, promptly grew up.

Such was the case again in *The Hell Cat* (1934), with Robert Armstrong and Ann Sothern. Armstrong was the hot-shot reporter, Ann the spoiled socialite who gets a job on the same paper. In due time, she sets out after some crooks and Armstrong has to help rescue her. Ah, but by now she's a true newspaperwoman and therefore worthy of his attention.

(It's entirely possible that the invention of the penniless socialite working as a newspaper reporter was a shrewdly calculated one. At a time when Middle America—or whatever the puritan belt was called back in the 1930s—still considered a woman's place to be in the home, a girl working in the rough-house world of male reporters might not be regarded as a respectable heroine. But if she were a nice girl,

from a well-bred family, who, through no fault of her own, suddenly had to earn a living, well, that could be a different matter, and she might not be so bad, after all.)

The battle of the sexes was even more forcefully joined in *Front Page Woman* (1935), which had Bette Davis and George Brent as reporters on rival papers, with Brent vowing to marry the girl if she ever quit "trying" to be a reporter, and Bette stubbornly out to prove she was as professional as he was. They even make a bet on the outcome of their rivalry: she promises to marry Brent if he catches the murderer before she does. But George Brent was never a match for Bette Davis — she solves the crime and marries him.

As usual, the B pictures were aping the bigger productions with smaller budgets. In 1932, Mae Clarke was a sob sister frustrated by the unreasonable demands of tough editor Pat O'Brien in *The Final Edition*.

In 1934, Claire Trevor played a sob sister in

Front Page Woman. Bette Davis is allowed to listen in on a vital development in her scoop. (Warner Brothers, 1935)

Hold That Girl, chasing after a gang of jewel thieves and having to be rescued by detective James Dunn.

A year later, James Dunn and Mae Clarke were rival reporters in *The Daring Young Man* (1935). And in 1936, Jane Wyatt was the fearless sob sister and Preston Foster the smitten detective in *We're Only Human.* Also in 1936, Claire Trevor was a socialite-turned-reporter in *Human Cargo* with Brian Donlevy as the seasoned reporter who falls for her.

One of the least likely female reporters of the decade was Joan Bennett in *Big Brown Eyes* (1936), in which she started out as a manicurist and was soon transformed into a newspaper columnist. Her leading man was

Cary Grant as a sharp detective who grudgingly accepts Joan's help in solving the crime.

But also in 1936, the same two stars were in *Wedding Present,* a far more diverting comedy that again played on the battle of the sexes, with both battlers as newspaper types. But with Grant as the city editor determined not to lose his favorite sob sister to a dullard of a suitor, the movie gave something of a hint of what was to come four years hence in another Grant comedy, *His Girl Friday,* about which more later.

Jean Arthur had a meaty role as a sob sister—with overtones of a Judas-type character—in Frank Capra's famous social commentary movie, *Mr. Deeds Goes to Town.*

Big Brown Eyes. Joan Bennett and Cary Grant solved a murder plus some personal difficulties. (Paramount, 1936)

Wedding Present. Back in the newspaper game were Cary Grant and Joan Bennett. (Paramount, 1936)

Mr. Deeds Goes to Town. Gary Cooper was the unsuspecting eccentric, Jean Arthur the furtive sob sister. (Columbia, 1936)

Editor George Bancroft assigns her to get an exclusive story on Gary Cooper, an eccentric millionaire who is spending his new-found money wildly. Posing as an unemployed secretary, she gains Cooper's confidence and continues to write sensational stories about him, until she finally realizes that (a) he's not so crazy, and (b) she's crazy about him. In the trial (to prove him insane) that climaxes the movie, it's sob sister Jean who speaks up in Cooper's defense, thus winning both the case and him.

Joan Blondell was the wise-cracking sob sister in *Back in Circulation* (1937) and Pat O'Brien was the whipcracking city editor, but they managed to work out their noisy differences.

In another of those socialite-taking-over-the-paper pastiches, cool Wendy Barrie was the neophyte publisher and Kent Taylor the furious editor. That was in *A Girl with Ideas* (1937), and it confirmed only that the writers of the script were without ideas.

That was also the year that the late Dorothy Kilgallen became a nationally famous reporter after she flew around the world for her New York newspaper. (In this case, life imitated the movies: Miss Kilgallen's father was editor of the paper.) But having thus attained fame, it was inevitable that she should appear in a movie, and as a newspaper woman. The

A Girl with Ideas. Wendy Barrie is the boss lady, Harry C. Bradley the old-time reporter. (Universal, 1937)

movie was a generally undistinguished newspaper-crime-scandal epic titled *Sinner Take All* (1937), and the stars were Bruce Cabot and Margaret Lindsay.

Despite the titular similarity, this should not be confused with an equally undistinguished 1939 movie, *Winner Take All*, in which Tony Martin played a guileless cowboy with a flair for fighting, and Gloria Stuart played—steady yourself—a sports writer who spotted his fistic proclivities, to say nothing of his heart.

Dorothy Kilgallen was not the only real-life newspaper woman to play herself in a movie. In 1938, Louella Parsons, then the queen of the Hollywood gossip columnists, lent her ample presence and her peculiar style of talking to a big Warner Brothers musical called *Hollywood Hotel*, which had Dick Powell, a couple of Lane sisters, and a small army of Busby Berkeley dancers.

And Hedda Hopper, that other hoydenish harbinger of Hollywood happenings, had made a number of screen appearances as an actress. But after she became Miss Parson's chief rival in gossip-mongering, Hedda played herself in several features, including *Sunset Boulevard* (1950), *Pepe* (1960), and *The Oscar* (1966).

By far the busiest sob sister of the 1930s was Glenda Farrell. As early as 1934, she had been the reprieved advice columnist in *Hi, Nellie*. In 1938, she was a newspaper photographer,

Back in Circulation. Joan Blondell and Pat O'Brien were feuding journalists once more. (Warner Brothers, 1937)

Sinner Take All. Bruce Cabot tries his press card on the officer, but Dorothy Kilgallen gets by with that half-smile. (MGM, 1937)

Hollywood Hotel. Dick Powell, Lola Lane, and Louella Parsons were among the principals in this musical. Miss Parsons played herself. (Warner Brothers, 1938)

coyly named "Click," in a quickie called *Exposed*.

But in 1937, Warner Brothers cast her in a harmless B picture called *Smart Blonde*. In it, she played a sharp-tongued reporter named Torchy Blane, who kept up a running battle with detective Barton MacLane.

The public response was healthy enough that the movie blossomed into a series. Late the same year, Warners released the second film, called *Torchy Blane, the Adventurous Blonde,* again with MacLane as Miss Farrell's foil.

Next in the series was *Blondes at Work* (1938), and after that Warners decided to drop the "blonde" reference and lean on the name

Torchy Gets Her Man. Glenda Farrell was Torchy Blane, seen here with Tom Kennedy.(Warner Brothers, 1938)

Torchy Runs for Mayor. Glenda Farrell makes a speech in front of a dubious audience including Tom Kennedy (in derby), Barton MacLane, and John Ridgley. (Warner Brothers, 1939)

value of Torchy Blane. Later in 1938, there was *Torchy Gets Her Man,* and early in 1939 it was *Torchy Blane in Chinatown.* Also in 1939, there was *Torchy Runs for Mayor.*

All five of these had Glenda Farrell playing Torchy and Barton MacLane as the tough detective who was soft on Torchy. But the studio must have had either difficulties with Miss Farrell, or else doubts about her. Because in the midst of this series with Glenda, the studio brought out two other Torchy Blane movies with different actresses playing the flippant reporter. In 1938, there was *Torchy Blane in Panama,* with Lola Lane as Torchy and Paul Kelly in the Barton MacLane part. And in 1939, the film was *Torchy Plays with Dynamite,* with Jane Wyman in the role of Torchy and Allen Jenkins as her leading man.

Perhaps the confusion was responsible, or maybe the series just ran its course. In any case, Torchy Blane was seen no more.

But there were still plenty of other sob sisters around to take up the slack.

Torchy Blane in Chinatown. The sob sister's most important weapon, next to her typewriter, was a phone, as Glenda Farrell demonstrates. (Warner Brothers, 1939)

In 1938, there was Rosalind Russell in *Four's a Crowd.* This was an Errol Flynn comedy in which the dashing Flynn played a newspaper editor who divides his love-making between heiress Olivia de Havilland and sob sister Russell. In this case, printer's ink was thicker than money and Flynn ended up with Russell.

Then there was *News is Made at Night* (1938), with Lynn Bari as the brash but green reporter and Preston Foster as the brusque managing editor. Despite their bickering they joined forces to save an innocent man from the gallows.

And in 1939, Joan Blondell and Pat O'Brien were back at it—feuding, fencing, and feeding each other lines—in *Off the Record,* again with Pat as the demanding editor and Joan as the mouthy columnist.

A year later, Claudette Colbert was a globe-trotting correspondent in *Arise My Love* (1940), but even though there was a harried, hair-tearing editor (Walter Abel), it was a war hero (Ray Milland) who won the lady's hand.

That year also gave us Eve Arden, almost a successor to Glenda Farrell in personality, as a funny foreign correspondent in *Comrade X,* competing with Clark Gable for a story. But even though Gable and Hedy Lamarr provided the romance, all three principals had some delightful dialogue supplied by those old hands at writing newspaper movies, Hecht and MacArthur.

One way and another, 1940 was a good year both for Hecht and MacArthur and for sob sisters. For that was the year their old tale, *The Front Page,* was dusted off, updated, and remade as *His Girl Friday,* with Rosalind Russell as the intrepid reporter, Cary Grant as the devious editor, and Ralph Bellamy as the hapless suitor. In this Howard Hawks film (scripted by Charles Lederer) Miss Russell just about perfected the Hollywood image of the indomitable girl reporter.

And it was also 1940 that brought us *The Philadelphia Story,* giving Ruth Hussey a good role as the girl photographer who accompanies James Stewart to the posh home of Katharine Hepburn to cover the big wedding. Although she was up against some high-

Comrade X. Sob sister Eve Arden comes between
Clark Gable and Hedy Lamarr in this scene. (MGM,
1940)

His Girl Friday. Hildy Johnson became a woman
(Rosalind Russell) in this funny remake of *The Front
Page.* With her is Ralph Bellamy. (Columbia, 1940)

The Philadelphia Story. Ruth Hussey sneaks some
candids in this scene from the Philip Barry play. (MGM,
1940)

powered talent, Miss Hussey managed to be noticed.

Barbara Stanwyck had a role similar to the Jean Arthur part in *Mr. Deeds Goes to Town* — that of a sob sister who falls in love with the man she's sneakily writing about — in the 1941 Frank Capra film, *Meet John Doe*. Once again, Gary Cooper was the victim of journalistic machinations, but love eventually conquered even Mr. Capra's passion for social commentary.

In the B picture field, Lynn Bari, who had been a sob sister in *News is Made at Night*, made it again in *Sleepers West* (1941), which was one of the Michael Shayne stories, with Lloyd Nolan playing the private detective.

Of greater importance, and quality, was the 1942 film, *Woman of the Year*, with Spencer Tracy and Katharine Hepburn. This witty movie gave Miss Hepburn a splendid role as a busy-busy syndicated pundit who marries earthy sports writer Tracy. Between dashing

Meet John Doe. Gary Cooper was the battered man of the title, Barbara Stanwyck the sob sister who invented him. (Warner Brothers, 1941)

News Is Made at Night. Reporter Lynn Bari and editor Preston Foster wore evening clothes to prove the title. (20th Century-Fox, 1938)

Sleepers West. Lloyd Nolan played Michael Shayne, private eye, and Lynn Bari was a reporter. (20th Century-Fox, 1941)

off profound think pieces, lecturing on world affairs, adopting war orphans, and other such portentous responsibilities, she has little time to be a good wife. When Tracy gets drunk and walks out on her, she even writes his sports column for him. But the woman in her finally responds to the man in him and the demanded happy ending is assured.

Barbara Stanwyck assumed substantially lighter duties in *Christmas in Connecticut* (1945). She was a columnist specializing in cooking and home-making, but her mean

Woman of the Year. Katharine Hepburn was more than a sob sister in this comedy-drama. With her is Spencer Tracy. (MGM, 1942)

editor assigned her to entertain a returning war hero (Dennis Morgan) to "get the story." What she got eventually was Morgan.

A more somber postwar film was *The Searching Wind* (1946) with Robert Young and Sylvia Sidney. In the past, Miss Sidney had played in films in which her leading men were newspapermen (Fredric March in *Merrily We Go to Hell;* Cary Grant in *Thirty Day Princess;* James Cagney in *Blood on the Sun)* but incredibly, she had never played a sob sister—incredibly, because when it came to sobbing, Sylvia Sidney took a back pew to no one.*

But she finally made it, and with a vengeance, in *The Searching Wind.* This being the first year after the end of the war, Lillian Hellman was one of the serious writers who began looking back with a bit of anger. Her screenplay (from her earlier stage play) concerned a rather stuffy American diplomat (Robert Young), his socialite wife (Ann Richards), and the girl he left behind: Sylvia Sidney. Young was one of those starry-eyed career diplomats who dismissed the threat of fascism, despite the public and histrionic warnings of alert journalist Sylvia. Miss Richards was the diplomat's shrewd wife who kept steering Young toward "safe" positions to protect his own career. Only when their son (Douglas Dick) became a war casualty did it dawn on Young that Miss Sidney knew what she was sobbing about, and that he had been partly responsible for creating the international climate that resulted in the war.

If Miss Hellman's script seems a little simplistic now, it should be remembered that this was at a time when America had just inherited the role of world leader and the twin sins of isolationism and appeasement loomed large in the minds of global thinkers. Whatever the merits of its message, *The Searching Wind* was an effective drama, and Sylvia Sidney was a convincingly wrought up sob sister.

But war or peace, the small budget factories still continued churning out stock sob sisters. In 1946, there was *Deadline for Murder,* with Sheila Ryan as the gutsy girl reporter, Paul

*In a 1974 interview, she said about those days: "Paramount paid me by the tear."

Christmas in Connecticut. Barbara Stanwyck was a
lady columnist, here with S.Z. Sakall. (Warner
Brothers, 1945)

The Searching Wind. Sylvia Sidney, the sobbiest sister
of them all, with Robert Young, starred in this Lillian
Hellman drama. (Paramount, 1946)

Deadline for Murder. Kent Taylor and Paul Kelly stand by as sob sister Sheila Ryan phones in her story. (20th Century-Fox, 1946)

Magic Town. Frank Darien, James Stewart, and Jane Wyman. Miss Wyman was the small-town editor. (RKO, 1947)

Kelly as the tough cop, and Kent Taylor as the wicked gambler. And in the same year, there was *Perilous Holiday*, with Ruth Warrick as the snoopy reporter and Pat O'Brien in the enigmatic role of a playboy type who was really after the bad guys, too.

In 1947, James Stewart starred in a Capra-less, Capra-type story, called *Magic Town*. Stewart played a public opinion pollster who found his Utopia: a small town whose residents reflected exactly the average for all

Perilous Holiday. Pat O'Brien, Ruth Warrick, Alan Hale, and Jay Novello. Miss Warrick was the reporter. (Columbia, 1946)

America. The place was called Grandview, and he went there with a couple of allies, Ned Sparks and Donald Meek.

Naturally, he must disguise his real mission, and naturally he meets Jane Wyman, the editor of the local paper—founded, just as naturally, by her late and revered father. She's all for progress in the town, which Stewart opposes for fear that a larger, more progressive Grandview would no longer be the "average town" so useful to his furtive polling.

Whatever weaknesses the script may have had—and they must seem fairly obvious by now—it's pleasant to report that Miss Wyman was a sufficiently resourceful reporter to pick up an extension phone and eavesdrop on one of Stewart's secret conversations, thus bringing the film to a long awaited climax.

Barbara Stanwyck plunged once more into the make-believe world of movie journalism in *To Please a Lady* (1950), with Clark Gable as her leading man. Gable was a racing-car driver and Miss Stanwyck a big syndicated colum-

To Please a Lady. Barbara Stanwyck was one of those
slick syndicated columnists, out to break Clark Gable.
(MGM, 1950)

nist. Whatever shortcomings Gable's role may have had, it was Gibraltar compared to the rickety part assigned Barbara.

She was one of those glib, sophisticated career women (like Rosalind Russell in the 1930s) who can dictate her radio column to a secretary and carry on a debate with her publisher, all while trying on stylish shoes.

For reasons that must have seemed supportable to the writers, Barbara is so appalled by Gable's reckless auto racing that she hounds him (via her column) out of his career, then pursues him until they fall in love. Oh, how the sob sister hath fallen.

Rather more palatable, though a minor effort, was *Washington Story* (1952), with Van Johnson and Patricia Neal. Johnson played a virtuous young Congressman who is attacked by a thoroughly slimy Washington columnist (Philip Ober). This prompts another reporter, Miss Neal, to try to find out for herself whether the legislator is a hero or a knave. She finds him blameless and also falls in love with him. That may not seem like the pinnacle of investigative reporting, but in those days of Washington probes into Hollywood's politics, it might well have been imprudent for a movie to suggest that a Washington politician might be less than incorruptible.

The year 1956 brought us that musical remake of *The Philadelphia Story*, titled *High Society*, one of whose delights was the win-

High Society. Frank Sinatra and Celeste Holm were the scandalmongers in this musical remake of *The Philadelphia Story*. (MGM, 1956)

ning performance of Celeste Holm in the role played earlier by Ruth Hussey. Like her predecessor, Miss Holm was surrounded by big names—Crosby, Sinatra and Grace Kelly—but she, too, refused to blend into the background.

Patricia Neal was a reporter again in a generally underrated movie called *A Face in the Crowd* (1957). The central figure was Andy Griffith as a totally amoral man, a guitar-strumming bum who becomes a big television star partly by climbing over the bodies of all in his path. Being human, Miss Neal goes through considerable soul-searching before taking a stand against this monster. Both stars performed brilliantly, and the film on the whole was a revealing examination of the fraudulent nature of popularity.

As with male reporters, however, the image of the sob sister had changed quite a bit between 1930 and the late 1950s. A 1957 example seems so anachronistic that it illustrates the point. This was *Beloved Infidel* with Gregory

Washington Story. Sob sister Patricia Neal tried to dig up some dirt on Congressman Van Johnson. (MGM, 1952)

154

A Face in the Crowd. Andy Griffith and Patricia Neal
are greeted by fans. He was a television star, she a
reporter. (Warner Brothers, 1957)

Beloved Infidel. If you could believe Gregory Peck as
F. Scott Fitzgerald and Deborah Kerr as Sheila
Graham, good luck. (20th Century-Fox, 1959)

Peck and Deborah Kerr. Based on the soapy memoirs of Hollywood columnist Sheila Graham, it told of that lady's unhappy affair with F. Scott Fitzgerald in the days when he was well on the skids. Neither star had much hope making a very favorable impression in this paperback movie.

As one further example of the decline and fall of the Hollywood sob sister, consider a 1968 horror entitled *Strategy of Terror,* with Hugh O'Brian and Barbara Rush. It featured a comic-strip plot about an attempt to destroy the United Nations headquarters in New York. O'Brian played a detective delivering a line about how he takes his coffee as if the line carried the weight of a Shakespearean soliloquy. Miss Rush was a girl reporter, knitting her pretty brow over the peculiar things happening around her. The villain was Harry Townes, equipped with crutches, presumably symbolizing his warped character, and saddled with lines like the one describing the UN as "A massive dedication to the undeserving."

Not once did Miss Rush do anything remotely suggesting the routine or the responsibilities of a newspaper reporter. One had the uneasy feeling that a command from her could no more stop the presses than Sydney Greenstreet could stop a slow grounder to third.

All of this explains not only why *Strategy of Terror* was such a dud, but perhaps why, by this time, the movie sob sister had become a patently endangered species.

Strategy of Terror. Reporter Barbara Rush looks uncomfortable in the presence of Harry Townes. (Universal, 1968)

8

EDITORS AND PUBLISHERS

When the movie version of *The Front Page* was released in 1931, its two stars, Adolphe Menjou and Pat O'Brien, were almost equally acclaimed. In fact, Menjou, who played the crafty editor, Walter Burns, got top billing, even though Hildy Johnson, the reporter played by O'Brien, was the "hero." This was undoubtedly because Menjou was then an already recognized star, whereas O'Brien was a newcomer to movies. Indeed, when Academy Awards for that year were made, Menjou was nominated as best actor, but O'Brien was not. As it turned out, the picture got three nominations but no awards.

In succeeding years, since the newspaper reporter was established as an attractive (or, at least, colorful) film hero, it stood to reason that he must regularly be pitted against his "natural" enemy: the editor. Walter Burns was depicted as a wily and ruthless manipulator of the destinies of his underlings, driven by the dictum that getting the story was more important than anything else and that this goal justified any means.

Considering, too, how many of Hollywood's newspaper movies, especially in the 1930s, were written by former newspaperman, one would expect a steady procession of managing editors, city editors, and publishers as ghoulish as the monsters who were then inhabiting the popular horror movies. What former reporter, grown bitter from years of having thick-headed editors mangle his deathless prose, could resist the golden opportunity to create the most unsavory fictional character imaginable and lable him "editor"?

Somehow, that didn't always happen. Some editors and publishers were shown in an unfavorable light. (Some were shown as out-and-out villains, but they'll be covered in another chapter.) But there were also editors and publishers in movies who were tolerably human, some even kindly and likable.

Perhaps because so many newsmen, at least in those halcyon days, used to nurture the dream of moving to a small town and running their own little newspapers—where, theoretically, nobody could tell them what to do—we've had a number of folksy, lovable, small town editors, presumably modeled on William Allen White, famed editor of the *Emporia* (Kansas) *Gazette,* setting type expertly, writing plain-talking front-page editorials that infuriate the town's starchy conservatives, spouting Socratic wisdom couched in horse-and-buggy language, possessing infinite patience and profound understanding of everything and everyone around them.

On the other hand, we've also had a parade of Walter Burns types, hard-nosed tyrannical editors whose chief concern was the welfare of the newspaper, and damn the torpedoes. And, in between, we've had some dashing, romantic editorial figures who devoted as much time to the battle of the sexes as to the battle of the deadlines.

Only a year after his screen debut as reporter Hildy Johnson, Pat O'Brien was elevated to editor in *The Final Edition* (1932). He was a tough one, too, who fired reporter Mae Clarke because she muffed a story. Mae then went about trying to solve a murder (there just happened to be one handy that needed solving),

The Front Page. The movies produced no more scheming editor than Adolphe Menjou, no matter how mild that punch Pat O'Brien is throwing looks. (United Artists, 1931)

The Final Editon. A year after his film debut, Pat O'Brien had moved up from reporter to editor. With him is Mae Clarke. (Columbia, 1932)

got herself trapped by the bad guys, and had to be rescued by tough but human Pat.

In the first of his several newspaper roles, Gary Grant was a New York newspaper publisher in *Thirty Day Princess* (1934). The princess of the title was Sylvia Sidney, who was actually leading a double life. Princess Sylvia was too ill to make a scheduled visit to the United States (to borrow money for her postage-stamp country) so an unknown actress—also played by Sylvia—is hired to impersonate her. And it is this ersatz princess that Grant meets and falls for.

By 1935, Clark Gable had already been a reporter twice in films: in the melodramatic *The Secret Six* (1931) and the memorable *It Happened One Night* (1934). Now he became

Thirty Day Princess. That was Sylvia Sidney, and Cary Grant was the publisher who fell for the ersatz princess. (Paramount, 1934)

the managing editor of a newspaper in *After Office Hours*, with Constance Bennett as his leading lady. Constance was a socialite (what else?) first fired by Gable, then rehired when he realized she could help him sew up a scandalous story about socially prominent Harvey Stephens. Despite the fusion of tough newsman and pretty socialite, as in *It Happened One Night,* this MGM movie wasn't in the same class with its famous predecessor.

The 1930s also brought us some of those folksy, small-town editors who seemed to appeal so much to the audiences of the depression days.

Will Rogers, at the peak of his career, starred as the editor of a one-man newspaper in *Life Begins at Forty* (1935), with Jane Darwell, Rochelle Hudson, and Richard Cromwell as the other principals. Between setting type and dispensing homilies, Rogers even found time to solve a crime. In fact, this was more a change of venue for Rogers than anything else. Most of his previous films had cast

After Office Hours. The smiling editor is Clark Gable and he seems happy to get Constance Bennett's story. (MGM, 1935)

him as a down-to-earth, seemingly unambitious soul who, in the end, seemed to know more than all the pretentious people around him, and so it was with *Life Begins at Forty*.

Warner Brothers, having witnessed the success of Rogers at Fox, made a feeble attempt to turn rotund Guy Kibbee into the same sort of lovable character. He was a folksy, small-town editor in something called *Mary Jane's Pa* (1935), which had Aline MacMahon fluttering her eyelids at the uneasy Kibbee.

Columbia's 1936 comedy, *Theodora Goes Wild*, with Irene Dunne and Melvyn Douglas, was about a small-town girl who wrote the *Peyton Place* of her time. When she began to

kick up her heels, there was a delighted hometown editor—in the person of Thomas Mitchell—who enjoyed reporting Theodora's escapades. The film has a good running gag in which Mitchell would receive, by phone or wire service, word of Theodora's latest romp, then turn to an aid and issue progressively outlandish commands: stop the presses, tear out the front page, get out that big bold type we used when the war ended, etc.

And in 1937 there was Paramount's comedy, *Wild Money*, based on a Paul Gallico story, with Edward Everett Horton running a small-town newspaper and tripping over a big story.

As was the case with reporters of the 1930s,

Life Begins at Forty. Jane Darwell, Rochelle Hudson, and Will Rogers ran one of those nice smalltown papers. (Fox, 1935)

Mary Jane's Pa. This time Guy Kibbee was the rube editor and Aline MacMahon gave him the eye. (Warner Brothers, 1935)

Theodora Goes Wild. And her home-town editor, Thomas Mitchell (at right), was delighted to print her exploits. (Columbia, 1936)

Wild Money. Lynne Overman, Benny Baker, and Edward Everett Horton were all involved with a small-
town paper. (Paramount, 1937)

there were editors whose romantic entanglements were really the meat of the movie, with
the career pretty much in the background.
Typical was *Wife Versus Secretary* (1936),
with Clark Gable, Myrna Loy, and Jean Harlow. It was an average triangle story, with
Gable as the publisher of a string of
magazines, Loy as the missus, and Harlow as
the fetching but innocent secretary. After the
usual number of feeble misunderstandings,
Gable and Loy are reconciled and Jean teams
up with a minor player who has been conveniently waiting in the wings for just such a
propitious moment.

No more substantial was *More Than a Secretary* (1937), in which George Brent was
editor and publisher of a health magazine
(called *Body and Brain*) when along comes
Jean Arthur to work as his secretary. But the
health magazine, it seems, is not enjoying
good financial health. So Jean lives up to her
billing in two ways: she helps save the
magazine from failure, and she also lands the
boss.

Miss Arthur had a far more impressive boss
in *Mr. Deeds Goes to Town,* also in 1936. This
engaging Capra comedy detailed the adventures of Longfellow Deeds (Gary Cooper),
who inherits a lot of money and is almost
adjudged insane because of the way he de-

Wife Versus Secretary. The secretary was Jean Harlow, and her publisher boss was Clark Gable. At right, Hobart Cavanaugh. (MGM, 1936)

More Than a Secretary. Magazine publisher George Brent and one of his lesser aids, Ruth Donnelly. (Columbia, 1937)

Mr. Deeds Goes to Town. George Bancroft's grin is meant to soothe reporter Jean Arthur. He was really a tough editor. (Columbia, 1936)

cides to spend it. Jean Arthur was the sly reporter who started out ridiculing Cooper in print (without his being aware of her true identity) and ended by falling in love with him.

The editor in the cast was George Bancroft, a big brute of a man who had been a leading man in earlier days and had, by now, gained much experience as an editor in films.

One of the movie's happier moments came when the tyrannical Bancroft was chewing out his staff for failing to stay on top of the news. The assembled underlings stood about docilely accepting this degrading scolding, but one of them lost his poise long enough to mutter an oath that was almost overheard by Bancroft — but was effectively denied the

audience by the simple device of the honking horn of a passing automobile drowning out part of his statement.

"What did you say?" demanded the angry Bancroft.

"Er. . . I said," stuttered the terrified reporter, glancing up at the editor's ceiling, "you've got dirty plaster."

Another interesting editor of the time was Spencer Tracy in the 1936 MGM comedy, *Libeled Lady.* Haggerty, the editor played by Tracy, was virtually on a par with Walter Burns. If he wasn't as witty, he was at least as fanatical in his devotion to duty above all else. When it became necessary to save his paper from a libel suit, he didn't flinch at having his

Libeled Lady. Editor Spencer Tracy has to con fiancée
Jean Harlow into marrying William Powell. (MGM,
1936)

fiancée (Jean Harlow) rush into a phoney marriage with William Powell, thus implying that
Myrna Loy, the lady about to sue for libel, was
herself guilty of playing around with a married
man.

(Ten years later, the same studio used the
same plot in a remake titled *Easy to Wed*. This
1946 edition had Keenan Wynn as the editor,
Lucille Ball as his fiancée, and Van Johnson
and Esther Williams as the romantic leads.
The best thing about the remake was Miss
Ball, a far more gifted comedienne than Miss
Harlow.)

While the major studios were casting their
Gables and Tracys as editors, the B picture
factories did what they could to keep pace.
From Universal, for instance, there was *A Girl*
with Ideas (1937), with editor Kent Taylor
forced to put up with the machinations of a
crafty publisher (Walter Pidgeon) on the one
hand, and the silly antics of the socialite who
had inherited the paper (Wendy Barrie) on the
other.

Miss Barrie was a newspaper owner again in
Newsboys' Home (1939) and didn't admit until
the last reel that her editor (Edmund Lowe)
could do a better job of running the paper than
she could.

Also in 1939, there was *They Asked for It*, in
which William Lundigan was the editor of a
paper in the kind of town where nothing much
happens—until the town drunk is found dead
and the man's daughter confesses to killing
him. Lundigan finds himself on top of a big

They Asked for It. William Lundigan (center) was the editor with a big story. At left is Michael Whalen. (Universal, 1939)

story and plays it for all it's worth, only to learn later that the confession was simply a phony attempt to grab publicity.

Another minor, but worthwhile, effort that year was *Tell No Tales,* with Melvyn Douglas as the managing editor of a newspaper about to fold. The story was routinely melodramatic — editor Douglas makes his own headlines by trapping a kidnap gang—but the movie's script and direction were good enough to keep the film moving along, and several of the characters were more than marginally interesting.

Then, in 1940, veteran director Howard Hawks took *The Front Page* and remade it — with a few twists — into a fast-paced, hilarious

Tell No Tales. Melvyn Douglas, the perfect editor, made his own headlines by capturing the kidnappers. (MGM, 1939)

comedy that yet retained the flavor of the original

The title was now *His Girl Friday*, and in that title was Hawk's basic switch: Hildy Johnson was now a girl reporter, played by Rosalind Russell. The Walter Burns role was placed in the capable hands of Cary Grant.

Changing Hildy's sex was an inspired idea, not only because Miss Russell was ideally suited to the role of a sharp, wise-cracking-proficient newspaperwoman. But the shift also gave the new version an added dimension: the running battle between Hildy and Walter was now a battle of the sexes as well, and although the sexual battle in newspaper offices had been done many times before——and would be done again——this Hawks film was a high point in the genre.

Additionally, switching Hildy to a woman made it necessary to make a man of the dullard to whom Hildy was betrothed. That role was tailor-made for Ralph Bellamy, then the screen's premier portrayor of ineffectual squares.

As for Cary Grant, he was an excellent Walter Burns, his own flair for farce being perfectly attuned to the role of the relentlessly tough editor. And the fact that Hildy was a woman, and a woman he loved (however reluctant he was to admit it) gave Walter Burns

His Girl Friday. The classic editor, Walter Burns, here played by Cary Grant, is more intent on his phone than on the argument between Ralph Bellamy and Rosalind Russell. (Columbia, 1940)

even stronger motivation for sabotaging her threatened resignation from his news staff.

Thus, using the cynicism of the original story, and spicing it with updated, sharp dialogue, Howard Hawks succeeded in getting the greatest value out of a classic and yet making it a contemporary (in 1940) film.

Incidentally, the role of Hildy in *His Girl Friday* was reportedly first offered to Claudette Colbert, who turned it down. But Miss Colbert played a newspaperwoman in another film later in the same year. This was *Arise My Love* (1940) and it was mostly a romantic drama—with the Spanish Civil War as a backdrop—involving Miss Colbert and Ray Milland. But it gave actor Walter Abel a good supporting role as one of those harassed

Arise My Love. Esther Dale brings editor Walter Abel a Bromo to calm him down. (Paramount, 1940)

Unholy Partners. Editor Edward G. Robinson and reporter William T. Orr join forces on a story. (MGM, 1941)

editors who keep screaming for some word from their far-flung correspondents— correspondents who, in movies, always seem to have far less sensitivity to the importance of deadlines than an understanding of the realities would sustain. But no matter. Abel was adept at conveying just the sort of impatience one would expect under the unlikely circumstances.

In 1941, Edward G. Robinson was an editor and publisher—and much more—in a minor MGM effort called *Unholy Partners*. Robinson played a veteran reporter who decided to start his own tabloid. To get financing, he is forced to accept racketeer Edward Arnold as his partner. Later, Robinson discovers that Arnold is blackmailing the girlfriend (Marsha Hunt) of his protégé (William T. Orr) and decides to do something about it. What he does is get into a lively argument with Arnold, which ends with Robinson killing Arnold in self-defense. There's not much left for a self-respecting editor-publisher to do then but take off on a dangerous trans-Atlantic flight with a conveniently mad pilot. The plane is lost at sea, Robinson's murder of Arnold is glossed over, and young Orr takes over the paper.

As with so many other hastily made films of the 1930s and 1940s—the days when the heavy demand for "product" helped producers to rationalize grinding out shoddy films—the newspaper background was no more than an excuse for a routine melodrama.

But 1941 also brought from Hollywood one of the finest of all newspaper dramas, and one of the best of all American films: *Citizen Kane*.

Much has been written in recent years about the disputed authorship of this boldly original movie, whether Orson Welles, who produced, directed, and starred in it, also wrote it unassisted. The screen credit for the writing lists the names of Herman J. Mankiewicz and Orson Welles, in that order. The former's champions have argued that he deserved most of the credit—and also that Welles tried to remove Mankiewicz's name from the credit list. It's interesting to note that although the film was nominated for Academy Awards in several catagories, the only Oscar it won was for its admittedly excellent screenplay.

In any event, *Citizen Kane* gave us one of the most fascinating newspaper characters ever to appear in films. Charles Foster Kane, whether or not he was closely modeled on William Randolph Hearst, as had long been commonly believed, was an arrogant, full-blooded, determined, complex man who spent much of his life asserting his will over weaker people, both in his personal relationships and in his publishing ventures.

However noble his motives may have been when he began to publish his first newspaper—and there's evidence in the film that vanity had a lot to do with it—he soon came to appreciate the power he had more than the use to which he put it. Kane used his newspaper power to promote a war in which he had no particular belief, he used it to attempt to legitimize his relationship with the young woman with whom he was caught in a "love nest."

Unlike so many of the superficial newspaper yarns that filled our screens over the years, *Citizen Kane* drew its drama not only from the personal conflicts of its leading characters but from the very way in which the handling of publishing power created some of those clashes.

One of the film's most touching moments climaxes the long-running conflict between Kane and his onetime friend, Jed Leland (Joseph Cotten). Leland, disenchanted with Kane's perfidy, has been transferred to Kane's Chicago paper, where he works as drama critic. When Kane's second wife (Dorothy Comingore) makes her disastrous operatic debut in Chicago, Leland is expected to write the review. Kane comes into the newspaper office, very late at night, to find Leland dead drunk, slumped over his typewriter, with the incompleted and scathingly unfavorable review still in the machine. In a characteristically grandiose gesture, Kane completes Leland's review — without in any way doctoring it — and prints it. Then he fires Leland.

Charles Foster Kane remains one of the most compelling of all film characters in a newspaper movie, and the Welles tour de force retains its magic several decades after it

Citizen Kane. Orson Welles, as Charles Foster Kane,
stands symbolically amid copies of his newspaper.
(RKO, 1941)

Citizen Kane. Everett Sloane and Orson Welles are
amused, but Erskine Sanford is fuming at what Kane
plans to do with his newly acquired paper. (RKO, 1941)

first appeared. If longevity is a test of art, then
truly *Citizen Kane* is an American work of film
art.

In 1974, when Orson Welles was chosen to
receive the American Film Institute's award
for life achievement, the citation said, in part:
"Orson Welles with one film influenced the
film art as much or more than any film maker
of our time. We honor him for his landmark
work on *Citizen Kane,* for the other memorable films he has written and directed, for his
work as a performer, and for the inspiration he
has provided to film makers the world over."

Not all editors in films have been as memorable. In 1946, for instance, William Gargan,
that B picture reporter of many years' experi-

ence, turned up in a minor item called *Night Editor*. But Gargan wasn't even a newspaperman. He was a dishonest cop who appeared in a flashback narrated by the night editor of the title—a minor role played by Charles D. Brown.

More relevant was the editor role played by Lee J. Cobb in *Call Northside 777* made in 1948. This better-than-average story of a stubborn reporter digging into a long forgotten crime had James Stewart in the leading role, but Cobb was quietly effective as the sympathetic editor who, despite some misgivings, allowed reporter Stewart to keep working on his crusading efforts to free an innocent man.

Night Editor. William Gargan (right) was a cop who turned crooked, remembered in a flashback by the night editor of the title. (Columbia, 1946)

Call Northside 777. While reporter James Stewart checks some facts, editor Lee J. Cobb awaits the results. (20th Century-Fox, 1948)

171

June Bride. No male reporter could accept happily the idea of working for a female editor. Thus it was with Robert Montgomery and Bette Davis. (Warner Brothers, 1948)

In 1948, Bette Davis was the slick editor of a slick women's magazine in *June Bride*, an entertaining comedy in which she was Robert Montgomery's boss.

In 1953, when Francis, the talking mule, staged his ludicrous invasion of journalism, it fell to Gene Lockhart to impersonate an editor. That actor of considerable ability was reduced to such tired admonitions as: "Get a story!"

The same year, Loretta Young and John Forsythe appeared in *It Happens Every*

Francis Covers the Big Town. Editor Gene Lockhart congratulates reporter Donald O'Connor, but it was really the mule who got the scoop. (Universal-International, 1953)

Thursday, which had to do with a husband and wife trying to run a small-town weekly paper. Most of the forced humor arose out of situations like finding one of their young offspring in a filing cabinet in the newspaper office.

Thomas Mitchell, who had fared well as the small-town editor in *Theodora Goes Wild*, was relatively colorless in *While the City Sleeps*, a 1956 melodrama that had Dana Andrews as the reporter and Vincent Price as a publishing tycoon.

But two years later, in 1958, Clark Gable, by now a veteran of eight newspaper roles, was a believable editor in a bright comedy called *Teacher's Pet*.

Gable played one of those confessedly uneducated city editors who snobbishly reject the alleged advantages of formal schooling in journalism. (And not too many years ago, such editors were more the rule than the exception.) Nevertheless, he is forced by his publisher to attend some journalism lectures at the local university, where he locks horns with one of the lecturers: Doris Day. In true Hollywood tradition, initial animosity promptly blossomed into undying love.

Even so, it was an enjoyable comedy and, as a kind of publicity-garnering stunt, the studio concerned (Paramount) imported a platoon of real newspapermen from around the United States and Canada to play themselves. They were sprinkled around the film's newspaper office, with virtually nothing to do but look authentic. But at least one critic found it reason enough to be pleased that none of these honest-to-goodness newsmen so much as uttered the hated phrase: "Stop the presses!"

Jack Webb, that television craftsman who popularized the staccato approach to crime investigation known as "Dragnet," delved into the world of the press in one of his few feature picture endeavors. This was in 1959 and the film was titled—succinctly but also cryptically—*30*. It was left for the uninitiated to find out for themselves that "30" is what newspaper reporters traditionally type at the end of a story.

Conceivably because the screenplay was by William Bowers, yet another former newsman who settled in Hollywood, the atmosphere of *30* rings relatively true, even though the drama

It Happens Every Thursday. That was when the weekly paper came out, thanks to husband-wife editors John Forsythe and Loretta Young. (Universal, 1953)

While the City Sleeps. Thomas Mitchell was the editor. With him are Vincent Price and George Sanders. (RKO, 1956)

Teacher's Pet. Tough city editor Clark Gable had to take some journalism courses from Doris Day. (Paramount, 1958)

30. Jack Webb was the busy editor in this newsroom drama. Behind him is William Conrad, television's "Cannon." (Warner Brothers, 1959)

is rather slower than was the case in earlier Webb efforts.

In a way, it followed the format of "Dragnet" and Webb's more recent television series, "Adam 12"— a day in the life of a metropolitan newspaper, in this case. When managing editor Webb, who also produced and directed the film, wasn't facing some editorial crisis, he was pondering the conflict between himself and his wife (Whitney Blake) as to whether or not to adopt a child.

The same year, *Lonelyhearts,* referred to earlier, gave us a colorful, if murkily drawn, managing editor in the person of Robert Ryan. This editor was a kind of sadist who divided his time between taunting his wife (Myrna Loy) about an ancient infidelity and needling lonelyhearts columnist Montgomery Clift over his naive compassion for his readers. Unhappily, even so skilled an actor as Ryan found it difficult to cope with the stilted prose provided by Dore Schary.

At the other extreme, that superb British actor Robert Morley gave us a thoroughly delightful portrait of an eccentric newspaper tycoon in the 1965 comedy *Those Magnificent Men in Their Flying Machines.* It was Lord Rawnsley, played by Morley, who sponsored the insane international aviation race that took up most of the film's time. And it was his daughter, played by Sarah Miles, who so infuriated the publisher by falling in love with the raunchy American (Stuart Whitman) who enters the race.

Those Magnificent Men in Their Flying Machines. They were put there by eccentric publisher Robert Morley, who sponsored the comic air race. His daughter was Sarah Miles. (20th Century-Fox, 1965)

Just as Jack Norton was typed playing drunks and Franklin Pangborn became the personification of the snobbish hotel manager, some actors spent much of their time playing editors. Whether the picture was a major production or a quickie, whether the script was gold or dross, they sat behind their desks, chomped on cigars or sucked on pipes, barked out orders to underlings, regularly fired or suspended heroic reporters, and usually ended up having to admit that George Brent (or Kent Taylor or Dennis O'Keefe or Michael Whalen) was worth stopping the presses for.

Among them were George Bancroft, Joseph Crehan, Charles Wilson, Thomas Jackson, Walter Connolly, Walter Kingsford, Henry Hull, Henry O'Neill, and John Litel.

Now and then, a supporting role as an editor would yield some fun. One that comes to mind was Don Ameche in *Love is News,* the 1937 romantic comedy with Tyrone Power and Loretta Young. Ameche was a pretty unlikely

Lonelyhearts. Wife Myrna Loy is used to editor Robert Ryan's cruel manner, but young reporter Montgomery Clift isn't. (United Artists, 1959)

Thomas Jackson. Another fairly busy editor type in a good many films.

George Bancroft. A formidable editor in many a film, from comedy to melodrama.

Joseph Crehan. As city editor or managing editor, he probably put more papers to bed than anyone else in Hollywood.

Roscoe Karns and Walter Connolly. Karns played countless reporters and photographers. Connolly was more often an editor or publisher.

city editor, riding horseback along broadway with Power, playing checkers with beer glasses on the tiled floor of a bar room, and otherwise indicating that occasionally editors can be as amusing as reporters—in the movies, at least.

Before closing this gallery of editors and publishers, a few women press executives come to mind. Generally, Hollywood has steered clear of women editors, perhaps because the concept of a female running a newspaper seemed too far out for producers, or possibly because other kinds of career women (lady lawyers, lady judges, etc.) were more obviously colorful. Besides Bette Davis in *June Bride* and Wendy Barrie in *A Girl with Ideas,* a few more are worth mentioning, if only to prove the species hasn't been altogether ignored.

Joan Crawford played a tough magazine editor in *The Best of Everything* (1959), a foamy drama about a woman who couldn't seem to find happiness at anything. Miss Crawford brought her customary authority to the part, but both the role and the glossy movie were unworthy of anyone's efforts.

And back in 1952, Samuel Fuller's film, *Park Row,* had given us a cardboard lady-editor publisher in the person of Miss Charity Hackett (Mary Welch). She was rich, snobbish, symbolic of the Establishment that Fuller's hero was out to fight. But mostly she was unbelievable.

Decidedly in the B category was a 1957 opus called *The Parson and the Outlaw,* another of the innumerable films dealing with Billy the Kid. This one merits mention here only because it had the relatively unusual gimmick of

The Best of Everything. Hope Lange was but one of the young employees driven by tough magazine editor Joan Crawford. (20th Century-Fox, 1959)

The Parson and the Outlaw. This Western was mostly
about Billy the kid, but Marie Windsor played a frontier
editor. (Columbia, 1957)

a lady editor (Marie Windsor) in the Wild
West.

But the film serves to bring to mind yet
another western involving a lady editor, and
quite possibly the least convincing newspaper
film ever made. Ironically, it fell to Claudette
Colbert — who had both played journalists
and been involved with a number of them in
her long screen career — to become an editor
in this pointless little film. The movie was
titled *Texas Lady* and was made in 1955 on
what must have been a meager budget.

Texas Lady, set in 1886, begins with Miss
Colbert, an impoverished belle of good stock,
beating gambler Barry Sullivan for $50,000 in
a New Orleans poker game. She uses her win-
nings to pay off an old debt of her late father's,
then heads for Texas to take over a small-town

paper she has inherited there. She runs into all
sorts of difficulties, from legal to violent, but
Claudette never gives up.

Actually, *Texas Lady* is really only a western, with the newspaper angle thrown in
primarily to get around having to use the standard justification for having a female star in a
western: the eastern school teacher.

But lip service is given to journalism, anyway. In the rustic little weekly newspaper office, for instance, there is a hand-lettered sign
that reads: "Don't tell it—write it!" But not
much heed is paid to such journalistic battle
cries.

Now and then, Claudette is given a bit of
business or a line to help remind us that she is,
after all, an editor.

An old timer—presumably the paper's sole

178

Texas Lady. Claudette Colbert was an unlikely editor in this oater. Barry Sullivan was her leading man. (RKO, 1955)

employee until her arrival—brings to her attention a report on Geronimo's death and asks casually if it should be run next to the railroad editorial. Editor Colbert, up to her hips in personal problems, manages to focus her attention on business long enough to reply, "Yes, that's fine."

On the off chance that you can't wait for this gem to turn up again on the television tube, it should be added that before long gambler Sullivan turns up, helps Claudette beat off the cattle barons, and declares his love for her. And in one of those stirring climaxes, the good people of the town, fully cognizant of the need for a free and healthy press in this backwater Texas town, pony up with the back taxes Claudette needs to save the paper.

Lone Star. Ava Gardner played at being a frontier editor in this big western, but the giddy poses of both Ava and co-star Clark Gable gives you an idea how seriously the journalistic aspect of the story was to be taken. (MGM, 1952)

Yet one more female Texas editor rates a mention. She was Ava Gardner in *Lone Star* (1952) and she had little to do but look gorgeous and wait around for Clark Gable to take her away from Broderick Crawford. But, let's face it, if there had been editors around who looked like Ava Gardner, very few of those newspapermen would have gone to Hollywood to turn screen writers.

9

THE NEWSMAN AS VILLAIN

For the first two decades of talking pictures, the American newspaperman was glorified, distorted, worshipped, satirized, and generally portrayed as clever, fearless, quixotic, intemperate, but somehow admirable.

In more recent years, as will be discussed later, the newsman has been subjected to sharper, less idealized, examination, and the verdict has not always been favorable.

But less-than-heroic newspapermen are not new, either. Although the overwhelming majority of newspaper films helped to forge the public image of the reporter as a kind of twentieth century folk hero—not without his little faults, mind you, but deep down a fairly decent chap—there have been notable exceptions to this practice.

The anti-hero is not so recent a concept in films as one might suppose. Writers of fiction long ago learned that villains could be far more fascinating than heroes, and that despite the notion that audiences must "identify" with a hero, the same audience could be moved to stronger emotional response by seeing a less likable leading man up there on the screen—particularly if he got his just reward by the end of the movie.

It sould also be remembered that from the beginning of newspaper movies, the emphasis was almost always on crime, scandal, and other wrong doing of the type that fills the less scholarly journals. Having exposed audiences to the notion that news reporters and editors could be so callous as to consider the story more important than the people involved in it—as was the case in *The Front Page*—it was only a short step onward to the belief, not totally unwarranted, that newsmen might be capable of using the power of the press for their own personal gain or selfish purpose.

An early example, indeed, was released a few months before *The Front Page* came out on film. This was *Scandal Sheet* (1931), with George Bancroft, Kay Francis, and Clive Brook. (The title was used at least twice again in newspaper films, but they were not simply remakes of the first story.)

Bancroft played the merciless managing editor of a scandal paper. He is shown as being so heartless that he feels no pity for those whose pecadilloes render them "good copy" for his yellow journal. Ah, but fate has a trick in store for him: somebody brings in a photograph of his own wife (Miss Francis) in a chummy pose with a prominent banker, played by Clive Brook.

After mulling this over for a relatively short while, Bancroft kills the offending homewrecker—so far, not an especially startling thing for a wronged husband to do in a movie. But next came the switch, the one that showed how dedicated even the murdering newspaperman could be: Bancroft, the printer's ink coursing through his veins, sat down and dictated the story of his crime for his own paper. Once the editon hit the street — scooping the opposition, naturally — Bancroft ended up in prison, where he was last seen, in this film, editing the prison newspaper.

Also in 1931, we had a more emotionally oriented "exposé" of yellow journalism in *Five Star Final*, with Edward G. Robinson as

Scandal Sheet. Editor George Bancroft (left) would stop at nothing for a story, not even murder. (Paramount, 1931)

the tough editor of a similar scandal sheet. But Robinson is not the sole villain of this picture. He is driven to his heartless action by the avarice of his publisher and the circulation manager. Hounded by them to boost the rag's readership, Robinson dredges up an old scandal, turning the glare of public exposure on a woman who had shot her husband twenty years before, had served her sentence, and was now living a blameless life. Robinson's scandal results in a couple of suicides and a great deal of crying.

Five Star Final also gave audiences an extra villain in the person of Boris Karloff, playing an unusually repulsive character who helps dig up some of the dirt on the hapless victims. Isopod, the character played by Karloff, is supposed to be a defrocked minister turned newspaperman—a sort of Rasputin become Winchell.

Five Star Final. Edward G. Robinson sent Boris Karloff, a clergyman turned reporter, on a scandal yarn. (Warner Brothers, 1931)

When Robinson fully realizes the consequences of his act, he loses his grip and tells off his boss. ("We're nothing but a pack of back-stabbing murderers" he shouts.) The publisher, stonily unmoved, fires Robinson.

The last scene of *Five Star Final* puts the scandal sheet in its proper perspective: a copy of the newspaper is shown being swept along a dirty gutter.

The theme of an editor being pushed toward greater circulation by a ruthless publisher was used again in 1932 in *Scandal for Sale*. The publisher, and, therefore, chief villain, was that past master at unctuous evil, Berton Churchill. His victim-accomplice was Charles Bickford, then at the height of his fame and always a capable actor.

Bickford was editor of the *New York*

Scandal for Sale. That's Charles Bickford on the phone, setting in motion an unsavory plot for his yellow journal. (Universal, 1932)

Comet, a new man on the job, so determined to prove his value that he neglected his wife (Rose Hobart) and burned the midnight oil in his attempts to build circulation. In her loneliness the wife turned for comfort to Bickford's star reporter, played by Pat O'Brien. Partly to help the paper, but also to rid himself of an unwanted rival, Bickford sent O'Brien on a reckless pioneer flight across the Atlantic. O'Brien was thus snuffed out, but not the story. It went on for a while yet, involving Bickford in further adventures. He was falsely accused of a crime, framed by some racketeers, and eventually exonerated.

One way and another, Bickford managed to enlarge the fortunes of publisher Churchill, so he was given a twenty-five thousand dollar bonus for his efforts. At this point, he quit his job and moved to Dayton, Ohio, a far, far better place, one was given to understand, than New York.

The villainous Mr. Churchill was again a hateful publisher in another movie of the era, albeit a much lighter one. This was *Friends of Mr. Sweeney* (1934), with Charlie Ruggles as the hero, a meek, intimidated reporter on a small-town weekly who falls prey to the traditional occupational hazard of all unhappy newsmen—booze—but with the result that he becomes emboldened enough to expose the town's crooked politicians, much to the chagrin of publisher Churchill.

In 1935, Spencer Tracy starred in *Murder Man,* in which he played an embittered newspaper reporter whose father and wife had been destroyed by a couple of unsavory types. By way of revenge, Tracy committed a murder and managed to pin the blame on one of his enemies (Harvey Stephens) convincingly enough that said enemy was found guilty and sentenced to death. Tracy then visited Stephens in prison for an interview—a singular display of gall that backfired, for Tracy ended up confessing his own guilt. Appearing opposite Tracy in this minor film was Virginia Bruce, playing a fellow reporter who managed to double as Tracy's conscience.

Women Men Marry (1937) was a B picture that went virtually unnoticed, although it was in some ways better than the aforementioned *Murder Man*. George Murphy was the report-

Friends of Mr. Sweeney. Charlie Ruggles was the timid reporter working for tyrannical publisher Berton Churchill. (Warner Brothers, 1934)

Murder Man. Spencer Tracy broods over his typewriter while Virginia Bruce consoles him. (MGM, 1935)

er in this one, working for editor Sidney Blackmer, another convincing villain of the time. In this case, Blackmer was carrying on an affair with Murphy's wife (Claire Dodd), but Murphy did not resort to any criminal means of disposing of his rival. Instead, the script provided him with a nice girl (Josephine Hutchinson) to wind up with when he realized that Claire was hardly worth fighting over.

The same year brought from Warner Brothers a fine movie called *They Won't Forget*, which dealt with the political realities of a Southern town shaken by a brutal murder. The central figure is an ambitious prosecutor (Claude Rains) who sees in the murder of a pretty high school girl (Lana Turner) a chance to propel himself into statewide prominence.

Women Men Marry. Cliff Edwards, Josephine Hutchinson, and George Murphy. Note the hats on and feet
on desk. (MGM, 1937)

They Won't Forget. Claude Rains (right) was the district attorney, Allyn Joslyn the local reporter. At left is
Donald Briggs. (Warner Brothers, 1937)

After examining his options—the black janitor of the high school, the murdered girl's boyfriend, the married teacher from up North—Rains settles on the last named suspect, knowing he is the only one whose conviction will satisfy the blood hungry town.

Not exactly peripheral to the story is Allyn Joslyn as the local reporter, observing the terrible drama around him yet privy to and going along with the prosecutor's scheme, helping whip the town into a frenzy, cynically wondering aloud, after it's all over, whether the convicted man was really guilty.

Apart from fashioning a taut and believeable melodrama, producer-director Mervyn LeRoy and his writers gave us something extra, a glimpse of another side of the newsman, as an observer, a force in the community, and yet part of the establishment, sensitive to what was "best for the community," rather than crying out for justice. This newsman had somewhat more depth than many of his predecessors in film, and the movie's indictment of his acceptance of the status quo was a far more serious charge than those usually offered in the superficial newspaper yarns of the early 1930s. He was also a type of newsman we were to see further developed and enlarged in subsequent movies.

But what made *They Won't Forget* memorable—apart from its skillful execution

Scandal Sheet. Otto Kruger was the merciless boss of a dirt-peddling tabloid, here with Ona Munson. (Columbia, 1939)

— was that it was the exception to the rule. Far more typical was *I Am the Law* (1938), a thin mixture of crime melodrama and newsroom shenanigans in which one of the villains was a newspaper woman.

The unlikely story had Edward G. Robinson as a law professor recruited by civic leader Otto Kruger to clean up the city's crime. This, it soon develops, is an uncommonly stupid move, since Kruger is himself behind much of the racketeering. As a further red herring, there's pretty Wendy Barrie as a newspaper columnist who has also, it seems, committed a murder. But good old reliable Eddie takes them all on and eventually unmasks all the villains, be they civic leaders, pretty columnists, or stock Hollywood hoodlums.

Otto Kruger, by then a familiar face in Hollywood films, had his chance to play a ruthless newspaper tycoon in *Scandal Sheet* (1939), another, even less successful, potboiler of the time. Kruger was a smoothly effective actor, but he had little chance to do much with the kind of stale situations afforded by this movie.

Edward Arnold, another accomplished movie villain of the era, fared much better in Frank Capra's 1941 movie, *Meet John Doe*. This was at the height of Capra's idealistic period, following on the heels of *Mr. Deeds Goes to Town* and *Mr. Smith Goes to Washington*.

I Am the Law. Wendy Barrie was a columnist with a murder in her past, Edward G. Robinson was a special prosecutor. (Columbia, 1938)

Meet John Doe. Edward Arnold (left) was the villainous publisher. Barbara Stanwyck, Gary Cooper, and Walter Brennan complete the group. (Warner Brothers, 1941)

It all starts with columnist Barbara Stanwyck inventing "John Doe" in a phony letter which she prints. This John Doe announces he is going to commit suicide on Christmas Eve in protest to man's inhumanity to man. When rivals accuse Barbara's paper of a cheap stunt, she is on the spot to produce John Doe. She finds him in the person of a down-at-the-heels smalltime baseball player, Gary Cooper. He is turned into a celebrity and John Doe Clubs spring up around the country. In time, Edward Arnold, the ambitious publisher of the paper, sees this as a golden opportunity and arranges for a huge John Doe convention at which he tries to coerce Doe into nominating him (Arnold) as a third-party candidate for the United States presidency. When Doe refuses, Arnold exposes him as a fraud. The only way Doe can prove his sincerity is to carry out Barbara's original threat—to commit suicide on Christmas Eve.

Doe is about to do this, but Barbara talks him out of it, and, in Capra's one relapse into happy-ending-Hollywoodism, even villain Arnold repents. But for most of the movie, Arnold's despicable villainy is superbly conveyed. And, incidentally, one of the joys of seeing this thirty-five year old movie is that it dispels the myth that Gary Cooper was limited to such monosyllabic utterings as "Yup."

Lee Tracy and Otto Kruger, two veterans of the news game in movies, teamed up in 1943

Power of the Press. Two newspaper veterans in the same movie: Lee Tracy and Otto Kruger. (Columbia, 1943)

for *Power of the Press*, which, unhappily, was just another go-around of the usual hoke about manipulation of newspaper power. It was almost as if the makers of this one had never heard either of *They Won't Forget* or *Meet John Doe*.

But a year later, Hollywood handed us a well-rounded newspaper villain in the person of Clifton Webb in the expertly made movie, *Laura*. This Otto Preminger film had no more message or meaning than a hundred other

Laura. Clifton Webb was the smooth villain of this well-made suspense film, playing a ruthless columnist. (20th Century-Fox, 1944)

murder yarns. What it had was style and class and wit, plus some good, meaty characters.

Chief among them was the role of Waldo Lydecker (played by Webb), a dandy of a smooth villain. Waldo was the nattiest of New York columnists, a sort of thin Alexander Woolcott. He was urbane, egotistical, devastatingly witty and mercilessly catty.

The story had to do with the brutal murder of Laura, a beautiful protégée of Waldo's. Assigned to the investigation is detective Dana Andrews, who eventually discovers not only that the girl whose head was blown off was not Laura but that the murderer is …Waldo himself. The generally commendable cast included Gene Tierney (as Laura), Vincent Price, and Judith Anderson.

But the parade of Bs continued. In 1946, Paul Kelly starred in *The Glass Alibi*, which involved an unscrupulous reporter who took a shot at committing the perfect crime and, of course, got caught. And in *The Underworld Story* (1950) newspaper publisher Herbert Marshall tried to aim suspicion at an innocent man in order to save his son from paying for a crime. But reporter Dan Duryea went in fighting and cleaned up the whole unsightly mess.

In between, there was *The Fountainhead* (1949), with Gary Cooper as an idealistic architect and Raymond Massey, dire and resonant, as a power-mad newspaper publisher. The whole film, from Ayn Rand's novel, dripped muddy symbolism.

But 1950 brought us one of the most successful and popular Hollywood films ever, the Joseph L. Mankiewicz classic, *All About Eve*. Although it is undisputably a Bette Davis vehicle (and one of her best), this brittle drama about Broadway types also offered a masterfully sketched villain named Addison DeWitt, for which portrayal George Sanders won an Oscar as the best supporting actor of the year.

In a discussion of the film, Mankiewicz has said that a first-rate villain can help make even the dullest of fictional heroes seem more appealing.

Addison DeWitt was one of those lions of Broadway, the columnist-cum-critic. But rather than being a mere observer of the story, he was pivotal to the plot of *All About Eve*. It was he who connived with the ambitious Eve

The Glass Alibi. Paul Kelly (in light suit) was the reporter gone wrong in this routine melodrama. (Republic, 1946)

The Underworld Story. Reporter Dan Duryea wasn't really the bad guy here, but it took him a while to prove it. (United Artists, 1950)

The Fountainhead. Idealistic architect Gary Cooper clashed with Raymond Massey, a publishing megalomaniac. (Warner Brothers, 1948)

All About Eve. Anne Baxter and George Sanders, almost equally villainous in his fine drama. Sanders was a Broadway columnist. (20th Century-Fox, 1950)

(Anne Baxter) to help make her a star, at Bette Davis's expense, and then, having done some quiet research into Eve's spurious background, was prepared to extract his reward in Eve's hotel room.

In a film that shone with brilliantly written and grandly played roles, George Sanders more than held his own as the sharp and pitiless Broadway sage. Unlike Waldo Lydecker, Addison DeWitt didn't kill anyone—but he was at least as cold-blooded as the role played by Clifton Webb in *Laura*.

Kirk Douglas was starred in *Ace in the Hole* (1951, and also known on television as *The Big Carnival*), surely one of the most brutal of newspaper stories in which the reporter is the villain. This Billy Wilder movie showed us a reporter (Douglas) so greedy for fame, so consumed by his own ambition that he is capable of turning a tragedy into a vehicle for his own glorification. The tragedy centers about a man trapped in a New Mexico cave, an event which Douglas promotes and prolongs with the aid of the poor man's amoral wife and an evil local sheriff.

The film was so unpleasant that more than one movie critic felt constrained to point out that few newspapermen would be that ruthless, and that, anyway, rival newsmen would never have allowed him to get away with it. (Shades of Bronx butchers bemoaning the way Ernest Borgnine held a cleaver in *Marty*.)

But in fact, Wilder, himself a former newspaperman and a sly cynic, was saying even

Ace in the Hole. Unscrupulous reporter Kirk Douglas threatens Jan Sterling in this sordid drama. (Paramount, 1951)

In 1952, we were treated to the third movie titled *Scandal Sheet,* this one with Broderick Crawford as the unprincipled tabloid editor who murders his own wife and then waits around to be found out. This one came from the prolific pen of Samuel Fuller, that onetime newsman who became a fountain of B picture newspaper yarns. The cast included John Derek and Donna Reed as young reporters, and Henry O'Neill as an older — and drunk — one.

more. In the carnival atmosphere of the town, waiting for the trapped man to die, Wilder was making a sardonic comment on the morbid curiosity of crowds—the same morbid curiosity, as a matter of fact, that helps sell sensational newspapers.

Only in his finale did Wilder slip. Perhaps because he had long since learned the rules of the Hollywood game, Wilder had his villainous reporter not only repent but plunge to his death. Even in 1951, the Production Code insisted on extracting its pound of flesh: villainy must not go unpunished.

The Big Knife. Ilka Chase was a vicious gossip columnist, Jack Palance played the movie star, and Paul Langton (right) was the studio head's flunky. (United Artists, 1955)

Scandal Sheet. Broderick Crawford was the merciless editor this time. With him is John Derek. (Columbia, 1952)

Hollywood chicanery was under the microscope in *The Big Knife* (1955), based on a Clifford Odets play. The sad hero was Jack Palance, playing a movie star who was tired of it all. Ida Lupino was his wife, who was tired of his philandering. Rod Steiger was the heartless studio head who ruled the destinies of his actors. Steiger was the chief villain, but he was ably assisted by Ilka Chase as one of those bitchy Hollywood columnists who thrive on the personal problems of the stars. It was a harsh, disconcerting film, clearly reflecting playwright Odets's disenchanted view of the movie capital. But if it missed as compelling drama, it at least gave us some vivid characters, not the least of whom was that cat played by Miss Chase.

But if Odets was disenchanted with Hol-

191

Sweet Smell of Success. Burt Lancaster played a hateful columnist and Tony Curtis was the ambitious press agent. (United Artists, 1957)

lywood, he was even more dismayed at the world of journalism in *Sweet Smell of Success* (1957), which dissected the seedy world of Broadway gossip columnists and the fawning press agents who live off them.

Burt Lancaster, of the lantern jaw and the toothy smile, discarded his usual style to give us a cool, restrained portrayal of the savagely power-mad Broadway columnist who can make or break anyone with a mention in his column. Tony Curtis, moving boldly away from the light comedies and inept swashbuck-

ling roles he'd hitherto relied on was equally impressive as the desperately eager press agent, willing to do Lancaster's bidding, a sweating, cowardly sycophant whose price tag was ever in evidence.

The columnist's wrath is incurred by Martin Milner as a young musician who has the audacity to attract the love of Lancaster's young sister. (There's a hint of incestuous yearnings on Lancaster's part, but that dramatic mine isn't explored too deeply.) The brutal columnist then sets out to destroy the offending musician and, predictably, is himself destroyed.

But the film was well written and directed, the key roles were admirably realized, and the texture of Broadway's seamier side was all too graphic.

In a quarter of a century of sound films, Hollywood's view of the journalist as villain had come a considerable distance—from the transparent knavery of George Bancroft in *Scandal Sheet* to the grotesque corruption of Kirk Douglas in *Ace in the Hole* to the abject megalomania of Burt Lancaster in *Sweet Smell of Success*.

The next fifteen years would bring forth yet more incisive portraits of newsmen, not necessarily as heroes or villains in the usual dramatic sense, but as representatives of some considerable force in American society — sometimes more sinister, sometimes more self-serving — as the public's perception of the press showed signs of change.

10
FINAL EDITION

In a 1965 movie called *Boeing, Boeing,* which had earlier been a stage hit, Jerry Lewis and Tony Curtis played rival foreign correspondents based in Paris. The story dealt mostly with the mix-ups created when Curtis's various girlfriends started turning up at unexpected and conflicting times.

In one scene, Lewis was called upon to comment that no newspaperman was ever inhibited by an absence of facts. The line got a laugh, but rather a mild one—probably because the audience regarded it as too old or too obvious a joke.

That bit of dialogue, and its casual acceptance by audiences, says a great deal about what happened to the public's image of newspapermen between the early 1930s and the 1960s.

In the days when newspapermen were widely regarded as modern American folk heroes, many a bar dispute could be settled (at least in the mind of one of the disputants) with a line like: "It must be true—it was in the papers." Not much more than a quarter of a century later, it had become more commonplace to hear: "You can't believe anything you read in the papers."

Just as Hollywood films had done much to mold the public image of the American newspaperman, they had a hand in planting the seeds of his destruction.

In the 1930s and 1940s, particularly, most of the reporters on the screen were one-dimensional characters, cardboard figures who made wisecracks, insulted their editors, outsmarted the police, and married the girl.

They were all pretty much the same, varying mainly by the degree of difference in the personalities of the actors who played them—Lew Ayres or Kent Taylor or Brian Donlevy or Pat O'Brien or Lloyd Nolan or Preston Foster or Wallace Ford or Dennis O'Keefe.

But during those same years, we had seen some far more interesting newspaper characters, and they were not always universally lovable.

Starting even with *The Front Page,* in which the newsmen's cynicism was the basic joke, and ranging through *Five Star Final, Libeled Lady, Nothing Sacred, They Won't Forget, Citizen Kane, Meet John Doe, Ace in the Hole,* and *Sweet Smell of Success* — to list only a few—we had met newspapermen who were heartless, shady, amoral, callous, brutal, criminal, reckless, and revolting. Very often colorful, it is true, but far from perfect.

Considering that uncounted millions of Americans had seen hundreds of these films, it would be foolhardy not to expect that a good many of them would have formed a skeptical view of what real-life newspapermen were like.

Added to that is the fact that the same people must also have noticed that there were times when real-life newspapers seemed to be behaving more or less the way the movies showed them.

Certainly, there have been scandalmongering papers that have hounded people. Surely, there have been many instances of stories being slanted, colored, or otherwise distorted to highlight a particular point of view. Obvi-

Boeing, Boeing. Tony Curtis (back to camera) and Jerry Lewis were foreign correspondents in Paris, up to their necks in girls. (Paramount, 1965)

ously, there have been reporters who have been sloppy, inaccurate, or even dishonest in their handling of stories. And, clearly, there have been editors and publishers more concerned with selling papers than with the responsible dissemination of news.

The newspapers could, one supposes, pass the buck right back to the public, arguing that sensationalism sells papers and if that's what the public wants that's what they're getting, but that view, whatever its shady merits, doesn't really absolve the press of its responsibility to provide fair and complete coverage of news.

To some extent, therefore, if the public's opinion of newspapers and their reporters had begun to go downhill over the years, both

Hollywood movies (many devised by former newspapermen) and some newspapers themselves must share the blame.

However, a couple of other factors probably entered into it, too, factors that would tend to further erode the public's faith in the press.

One was certainly the growth of television, from about 1950 on. It's interesting to note, incidentally, that in those early days of television, there were several attempts at presenting programs dealing with newspapermen —and dealing with them rather favorably, too.

One of the first was a series called "Big Town," in 1950. This had already been a popular radio series, with Edward G. Robinson as the crusading editor and Claire Trevor as his aid. On television, Mark Stevens played Steve

Wilson, the editor, and the girl was played by Jane Nigh.

The same year, Harold Huber (hitherto a B picture gangster) played a New York columnist in a television series called "I Cover Times Square." At about the same time, Edmund Lowe was starred as a crime-busting columnist in a series titled "Front Page Detective."

In 1952, there was "Crime Photographer," another weekly television series, with Darren McGavin playing the title role, and a few seasons later Charles Bronson was starred in a series called "Man with a Camera." In between came "Wire Service" (1956), with two veteran movie newsmen: George Brent and Dane Clark. Also in 1956, there was "Big Story," with radio veteran Ben Grauer as host, which dramatized actual news stories and saluted the various crimebusters or crusaders who had broken the big stories.

And our old friend, the advice-to-the-lovelorn columnist, had a shot at television fame, too. This was in a comedy series called "Dear Phoebe," begun in 1954, with Peter Lawford as the updated Nellie.

It may be a commentary on the public's attitude toward newspaper heroes—or, possi-

Peter Lawford. The advice-to-the-lovelorn column was revived once more for a television series called "Dear Phoebe," in which Lawford starred.

bly, on the quality of television shows—that not one of the above-named series can be regarded as raging successes. Most of them lasted a year or two and were canceled; some were syndicated, station by station and never had a chance to grab a big network following.

It may also be a commentary on the taste of television audiences that there was one successful television series about a newspaper reporter. He was mild-mannered Clark Kent, who had the peculiar habit of stepping into a phone booth, stripping down to his red long-johns, and masquerading as Superman in order to outsmart an endless parade of comic-strip villains. The series was popular mostly with children and lasted for several years.

But the growth of television—evidently not because of any of the aforementioned sterling series about newsmen—created something of a problem for many newspapers, both large and small.

Darren McGavin. Star of the early television series "Crime Photographer."

A generation before, when radio was becoming a national craze, a good many newspapers took the singularly unrealistic position that if they ignored it, it might go away. Radio was, after all, a competitor, for not only was it carrying news broadcasts but it was also competing for advertising dollars, which hitherto had been spent mostly in newspapers and magazines.

In time, the folly of this attitude became obvious to even the most stubborn editors, and the printing of radio program listings and even radio news and reviews became an accepted policy on most big newspapers.

Now, in the early 1950s, a new monster had appeared to threaten the smooth and profitable running of the presses: television. It was a threat in two ways. First, it attracted advertising dollars, as radio had done. Secondly, it competed with movies—urging people to stay at home and watch television programs rather than go out to pay for movies—and the movie advertisers weren't too anxious to see newspapers, where they spent money advertising their films, cover television.

Again, the newspaper dilemma: should editors give space to this healthy new youngster that threatened to grow up into a great big rival? Once again, too many papers took the ostrichlike position they had in the radio days. This, in turn, prompted television to become unfriendly toward newspapers.

One area where this became evident was in the "talk shows" that began to blossom by the mid-1950s. Jack Paar, at the height of his popularity as host of NBC's "Tonight Show," had various running feuds with an assortment of columnists and newspapers—from Walter Winchell to the *New York Times*.

Paar and other talk-show hosts did something further: they provided a forum for actors, performers, politicians, authors, and other notables to talk back to newspapers that had criticized them. Paar's position, perhaps not unreasonably, was that if the press had the freedom to criticize him, he should have the same freedom to criticize the press.

But Paar wasn't alone. David Merrick, the highly successful and decidedly shrewd Broadway producer, spent a good bit of his time in publicly denouncing the press

—particularly the theater critics, but also the press generally. Whenever one of his shows got unfavorable reviews (and not all of them did) Merrick would turn up on a television talk show and make extravagant charges that all newpapermen were prostitutes who could be bought off for a bottle of booze. If he was in Cleveland, he would announce that Cleveland had the worst drama critics in America. If he was in Detroit or St. Louis or any other major city, he would make similar charges about that city's critics.

Television, of course, delighted in fanning the flames, and Merrick was a familiar figure on talk shows. In addition, a lot of newspapers showed their masochistic side by printing these rash attacks against them by Merrick and other irate producers, entrepreneurs, actors, or politicians.

With millions of viewers watching Jack Paar, Arthur Godfrey, David Susskind, and other television personalities who did not shy away from feuds with the press, and with newspapers sometimes falling into the trap of knocking everything on television (not only those who attacked the press) as a means of disenchanting the public with television in general, the public's attitude toward newspapers was bound to become even more jaded.

And what was Hollywood doing during all this?

One can't always be certain whether filmmakers anticipate (and therefore shape) public taste or just wait and follow it. In this instance, there seems to be evidence of both, which may mean neither.

In any case, the 1950s gave us such unwholesome newspaper people as Kirk Douglas in *Ace in the Hole*, Ilka Chase in *The Big Knife*, and Burt Lancaster in *Sweet Smell of Success*. There had been journalistic heels earlier, of course, but they did seem to be getting worse.

A newer kind of non-hero representing the world of journalism on the screen was the impassive observer who declined to use his position of power (a column or an editorial) to denounce evil or injustice when he tripped over it.

One such example was the role played by

The Great Man. Keenan Wynn rants while Jose Ferrer
listens. Ferrer was a journalist stymied by the system.
(Universal, 1957)

Jose Ferrer in *The Great Man* (1957). Ferrer was a radio journalist assigned to assemble a tribute to a recently deceased radio idol. As he delved into the great man's background, he found just the opposite of what he had expected: the radio idol had been an unmitigated heel who had clawed his way to fame, destroying anyone in his path. Ferrer eventually came into conflict with Keenan Wynn, the fallen idol's ex-manager, who was determined to preserve the clean image of his one-time client. Ferrer tried, half-heartedly, to fight Madison Avenue forces that didn't want the dead star's image tarnished, but in the end they defeated him, the legend of the great man was perpetuated, and Mr. Ferrer came off as an impotent champion of truth. (None of this is intended to suggest *The Great Man* was not a good film; it was.)

In 1958, Susan Hayward starred in *I Want to Live,* another first-rate film dealing with the downfall of a reckless woman who drifts from petty crime to petty crime and is finally charged with a murder she did not commit. Playing a key role in the film was Simon Oakland as a newspaper reporter who first helped to build the hysterical public case against her, and then reversed himself and fought to save her from the gallows. By the end of the film, Oakland, gradually convinced he had made a bad mistake, is a sympathetic but powerless witness to Miss Hayward's destruction. But the audience is left with the unmistakable feeling that if he had been a better reporter to begin with—and one more interested in justice than newspaper headlines—the lady would be alive and free.

The film was a great success, winning an

I Want to Live. Susan Hayward, bound for prison, blames reporter Simon Oakland for her troubles. (United Artists, 1958)

Academy Award for Miss Hayward. The story of Barbara Graham, the character she played, was based on a true one. And the character played by Oakland was real, too, thereby lending more credence to the strongly projected view that an irresponsible newsman can be guilty of crucifying an innocent person.

No moviegoer could miss the point of the message in a line hurled at Oakland by Miss Hayward as she went to prison: ''You chewed me up in your headlines. All the jury had to do was spit me out!''

The impotent—not to say unfeeling—observer was again represented in the 1960 film, *Elmer Gantry,* based on the fascinating old novel by Sinclair Lewis, and with Burt Lancaster in the title role. In this film, Arthur Kennedy played a reporter who watched at close range and without objection the rise of the flamboyant (and phony) evangelist created by Lewis and considerably muddled by the short-cuts of the movie. The Kennedy role was reminiscent of one played by John Ireland in *All the King's Men,* as a reporter who

Elmer Gantry. Arthur Kennedy played a reporter who watched more or less impassively, while the evangelist rose to fame. (United Artists, 1960)

watched the rise of a demagogue (Broderick Crawford), but whereas the reporter in the earlier film seemed to have some sense of having backed the wrong horse, Kennedy sits by and watches Lancaster grow, never once taking the evangelist's "faith" seriously, but also never doing anything to expose him —clearly, a journalistic sin of omission.

H.L. Mencken, one of the towering figures of American journalism, was vaguely impersonated as a secondary character in *Inherit the Wind* (1960), the Stanely Kramer production of a previously acclaimed stage hit. The primary characters were modeled after William Jennings Bryan and Clarence Darrow, and their battleground was the famous Scopes "monkey trial" of 1925.

Of course, all the names were changed (even Scopes became Cates) to protect the sensitive. Darrow was called Drummond, Bryan was Brady, and H.L. Mencken became E.K. Hornbeck. The film was an outstanding success, the confrontation between the two famous lawyers being only slightly more electrifying than that between the two dynamic actors who played them: Spencer Tracy as Darrow and Fredric March as Bryan. But Mencken (or Hornbeck), as interpreted by Gene Kelly, was almost lost in the shuffle. He was a cynical observer of the carnival going on around him, but somehow not very much of what he said was up to the Mencken level.

Two considerably more villainous reporters turned up in films the following year. One of these was in *The Hoodlum Priest,* based on the experiences of a real Jesuit priest, Father Charles Dismas Clark, in trying to straighten up youthful criminals. As played by Don Mur-

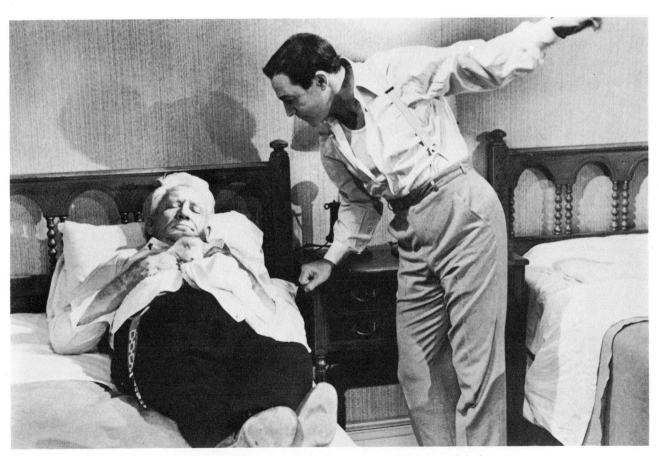

Inherit the Wind. Spencer Tracy's role was modeled after Clarence Darrow, and Gene Kelly represented a watered-down H.L. Mencken. (United Artists, 1960)

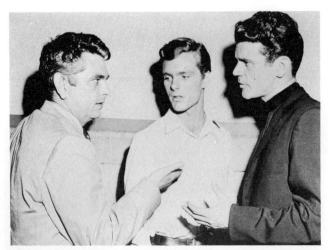

The Hoodlum Priest. Priest Don Murray was trying to help young criminal Keir Dullea. But reporter Logan Ramsey (left) fought him all the way. (United Artists, 1961)

ray, the priest comes off as a compassionate and courageous man with considerable faith in rehabilitation. Representing youth gone wrong was Keir Dullea and he, too, gave an impressive performance.

The closest thing to a villain was Logan Ramsey as a newspaper reporter who refused to believe either in what Father Clark was trying to do or even in the priest's sincerity. It was difficult, from the standpoint of the audience, not to regard Ramsey as a destructive meddler.

The Mark. Donald Houston was the scandal-seeking reporter who helped complicate the plot of this serious drama. (Continental Distributing, Inc., 1961)

Even less likable was the part played by Donald Houston in another 1961 film, *The Mark,* which starred Stuart Whitman and Rod Steiger.

This engrossing film took on the rather delicate subject of the rehabilitation of an emotionally disturbed man (Whitman) who had served a prison term for assaulting a little girl. Steiger played the tough but understanding psychiatrist who devoted his time to helping Whitman in his uphill struggle toward mental health.

The monkey wrench was recklessly wielded by a snoopy reporter (Houston) who doggedly dug up Whitman's past record and insisted on hounding this already troubled man. If ever a movie reporter was gratuitously guilty of invasion of privacy, this was the one.

Not all films dealing with newspapermen in the 1960s were tough on the press. In 1965, the same year that Jerry Lewis made his glib comment about newspapermen never being inhibited by an absence of facts (in *Boeing, Boeing),* a far more sensitive reporter was played by Sidney Poitier in *The Bedford Incident.*

Richard Widmark was the skipper of the *Bedford,* an American destroyer patroling the North Atlantic. For some unlikely reason, Poitier, as a magazine reporter, had been allowed aboard for this journey and he spent much of the film getting into Widmark's hair.

But Widmark was a strange case. Like some futuristic Captain Ahab stalking an alien Moby Dick, he seemed determined to track down a Russian submarine whose behavior he regarded as suspicious. So keyed up did he keep his crew that the inevitable happened: signals got mixed, a panic button was pushed and, presumably, the world was plunged into an accidental nuclear war.

What the movie seemed to be trying to say was that the practice of brinksmanship is a horrible risk and the future of the world should not be left in the hands of such hotheads as Widmark. If it was also suggesting that a free and vigorous press could act as a brake on such excesses, the point got lost in the explosion.

In 1967, Richard Brooks (who had earlier been responsible for *Deadline, U.S.A.* and

The Bedford Incident. Richard Widmark, Eric Portman, and Sidney Poitier aboard the *Bedford*. Widmark was the skipper, Poitier a curious journalist. (Columbia, 1965)

Elmer Gantry, among others) wrote and directed the screen version of Truman Capote's justly famous book, *In Cold Blood.* Like the book, the film was a detailed examination of the horribly violent crime committed by two drifters in Kansas back in 1959.

Although the story became known nationally through the efforts of novelist-turned-journalist Capote, the reporter in the film (played by Paul Stewart) is a minor character.

In Cold Blood did a rather curious thing. After proving to us abundantly the guilt of the two young killers (Robert Blake and Scott Wilson), it set out to elicit our sympathy for them when they were about to be executed for their crime. Perhaps this seeming ambival-

ence was the intention of Capote and Brooks, leaving the audience with the uncomfortable feeling that however revolted society might be by violent crime the action of society in extracting its maximum penalty was equally barbaric.

In any event, Mr. Stewart's reporter barely hinted at such sentiments, testing gingerly the uncharted waters of opposition to capital punishment.

By now, violence and crime in America had become a big enough issue that those opposed to the death penalty were often suspect. There were cries from politicians about the "coddling" of criminals and charges that the police were being hampered in their efforts to reestablish law and order by slippery lawyers and, more seriously, by indulgent courts.

Reflecting this attitude was a 1969 film titled *Company of Killers*, in which newspaper reporter Clu Gulager had some difficulty in deciding whether the police were the white hats or the black hats. Essentially, this was a crime detection film, but the point (the police's point) was made abundantly clear to the representative of the press: either you're with us or against us. Detective Van Johnson kept hammering home this argument, along with periodic lectures about the newspapers giving the police "the wrong kind of publicity," until Gulager finally got the message and accepted police goals as being more important than journalistic independence.

Against a different backdrop, much the same message had been used on foreign correspondent David Janssen in *The Green Berets* (1968), until the "facts" forced him to abandon his neutralist position and plunge whole-heartedly into the hawks' nest.

In a lighter vein, also in 1969, Norman Jewison produced and directed *Gaily, Gaily,* a colorful, lusty, and nostalgic yarn once again from the prolific pen of Ben Hecht. A throwback to Hecht's youth, it told of a callow youth who turned up in Chicago in the gaslight era and tumbled into a succession of bawdy adventures involving prostitutes, corrupt

politicians, hard-drinking newspapermen, and the like. Beau Bridges was the young man, Brian Keith was the hardened newsman who had a soft spot in his heart for Melina Mercouri, a madam of pure gold.

Hecht's (and Jewison's) treatment of newspapermen was certainly irreverent, but they emerged at least as lovable scamps—rather like the ones in *The Front Page* — rather than meddling boors. Although the film was not a notable success, it had some fine moments of high comedy.

By this time—the start of the 1970s — another factor had entered into the public's consciousness that would affect its feelings toward the press, or, to use the term that had become current, "the media."

(One lamentable result of the growth of television has been the lumping together of all means of communication under the leaky umbrella called "the media." Worse still is the sloppy habit some politicians and commentators have fallen into of using the word as if it were singular rather than plural: "The media is...")

Spiro Agnew, then the vice-president of the United States, launched into what turned out to be not just a one-man campaign against the "excesses" of something called the "liberal Eastern Establishment" wing of The Media. It later developed that some of his alliterative rhetoric (i.e., "nattering nabobs of negativism") were the work of one Patrick Buchanan, a White House speech writer.

It may be useful to remember, incidentally, that the Nixon administration's battle with "the media" began well before the famous Pentagon Papers were stolen and released to the *New York Times*, that bastion of the "liberal Eastern Establishment" which had, in fact, supported Mr. Nixon for the presidency in 1968 and was to do so again in 1972.

Agnew had yet another ally, Clay T. Whitehead, one of that army of special assistants surrounding Mr. Nixon. He took a special interest in television and began questioning whether it was fair that news should be "controlled" by the three national television networks.

Thus the stage was set for a rambling national debate that was to go on—or on and

Gaily, Gaily. Brian Keith (center) was the hard-drinking newsman, and Beau Bridges (right) his young protégé. (United Artists, 1969)

off—for several years, during which time one heard, again and again, that the liberal or radical press (Agnew even managed to combine them with a wide brush called "radicalib") was unfair to the president, the politicians, the police, and all those others who stood for the return of Law and Order.

If all this seems tangential, it should be pointed out that the White House's battle with "the media" was surely calculated to have an effect on the public's evaluation of the press—which, in turn, would just as surely have an effect on what kind of newspaper movies, if any, film makers might be tempted to make.

In view of what took place later, it was almost as if Mr. Nixon and all those special assistants were preparing the American public for the worst by hammering away at that revealingly protesting slogan—Don't Believe What You Read in the Papers—just in case something should happen.

And, of course, something did happen. It came to be known as Watergate, and, in time, it was to cause the pendulum to start swinging the other way—barely perceptibly at first, perhaps, but still a start. Because it turned out that a great deal of what the press (nay, the media) had been saying about Mr. Nixon and his "overzealous but dedicated" aides was substantially true.

It began with two young police reporters on the *Washington Post*—almost like the plot of a 1937 B picture—who were permitted to dig deeper into what the White House kept insisting was nothing more than a third-rate burglary.

It resulted, two years later, in the ignominious resignation of Mr. Nixon after he had admitted to his stunned supporters on the House Judiciary Committee that some of his previous statements on Watergate had not been entirely accurate. He had, in fact, aided and abetted the famous cover-up.

Suddenly, something called "investigative reporting" had become respectable again. Other large newspapers (the *New York Times*, the *Los Angeles Times*) and magazines (*Newsweek, Time*) sent platoons of reporters to dig still deeper, and gradually a staggering case was built—and publicized by the media—against the Nixon duplicity, until even the staunchest supporters could no longer fall back on the feeble argument that the liberal Eastern Establishment wing of the media was persecuting the president.

Meanwhile, the two *Washington Post* reporters, Carl Bernstein and Bob Woodward, had already brought out a book on Watergate, titled *All the President's Men.* And even before the book came out (to become a nationwide best-seller) the movie rights were snapped up by Robert Redford.

Ironically, that film, released in the spring of 1976 by Warner Brothers, turned out to be one of the finest newspaper movies ever made. With Redford as Woodward and Dustin Hoffman as Bernstein, *All the President's Men* dispensed with the decrepit clichés of old-time newspaper films and gave us instead an engrossing depiction of how real reporters function.

Moreover, it did so without sacrificing any of the stunning impact of the biggest political scandal in modern American history. No smart-ass reporters hurling insults at their editors, no fisticuffs with the bad guys, nobody yelling "Stop the Presses!" In their place, we saw two serious, determined, hard-working newsmen plodding, digging, cajoling for every last bit of publishable detail that would ultimately link the Watergate burglary to the Oval Office of the White House.

It was like a classic detective story told in dramatic rather than melodramatic language, and it did more to improve the image of the press than any film in the past two decades.

One movie, however, does not a trend make. It remains to be seen whether other forthcoming films will reflect any return to respectability, in the public's mind, for the minions of "the media."

In any event, the reporter was still turning up in occasional films, though hardly with the frequency of earlier decades. A look at some of them suggests no discernible unanimity of viewpoint as to the legitimacy of the press's role in society.

Early in 1974, for instance, Maximilian Schell wrote, produced, directed, and played a supporting role in a film titled *The Pedestrian.* It dealt with an aging German indus-

The Pedestrian. Peter Hall (center) was a scandal-seeking newsman bent on exposing a former Nazi. (Cinerama, 1974)

trialist (Gustav Rudolf Sellner) trying to live out his life in peace and forget his part in the Nazi nightmare. But he is hounded by a scandalmongering editor (Peter Hall) who is determined to dig up the past and destroy the old man. The film failed to attract much attention when it opened, despite some good reviews.

In the summer of 1974—virtually at the time Mr. Nixon was making his dramatic departure from Washington—a film called *The Girl from Petrovka* opened. Starring Goldie Hawn and Hal Holbrook, this romantic comedy-drama was almost a throwback to the 1940s, a cross between *Comrade X* and *Somewhere I'll Find You*. Miss Hawn played a young Russian ballerina and Holbrook was that familiar figure, the American foreign correspondent in Moscow who falls for the pretty Russian girl.

Despite lukewarm reviews, *The Girl from Petrovka* had something else going for it, the film was riding the crest of a continuing trend called nostalgia. After the success of such films as *The Last Picture Show, Paper Moon, American Grafitti, The Way We Were, The*

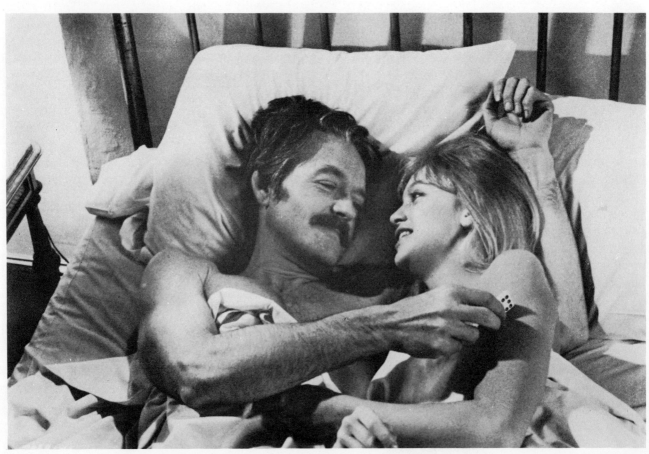

The Girl from Petrovka. Overseas correspondent Hal Holbrook takes a little time off duty with Goldie Hawn, who plays a Russian ballerina. (Universal, 1974)

Sting, and *Chinatown,* nostalgia with all the stops out was very much in order.

It was no mere coincidence, therefore, that 1974 was also the year of another remake of the Hecht-MacArthur prototype, *The Front Page.* This time around, Jack Lemmon played Hildy Johnson and Walter Matthau was Walter Burns. Wisely, director Billy Wilder, an old hand at Lemmon-Matthau collaborations, retained the original era (the 1920s) and flavor.

A different approach to nostalgia might explain the appearance, also in 1974, of a film called *The Odessa File.* Based on the successful novel by Frederick Forsyth, it was a throwback to the old-fashioned kind of movie reporter (hardly distinguishable from the private eye) who gets so involved in a story that he loses sight of the fact that he's supposed to get a story rather than apprehend the bad guy. The reporter in this case is a German freelance (ably played by Jon Voight) who trips over knowledge of the existence of a secret organization in which former SS men hide. In the course of tracking down his story, Voight is beaten up, thrown in front of a subway train, stalked by a killer, etc. There's a good deal of suspense in the first two thirds of the movie, but it slips into some rather trite situations towards the end, including the melodramatic revelation that the crypto-Nazi being pursued by Voight (Maximilian Schell) was the very man who murdered Voight's father.

Far more contemporary, at least superficially, was Alan Pakula's 1974 thriller, *The*

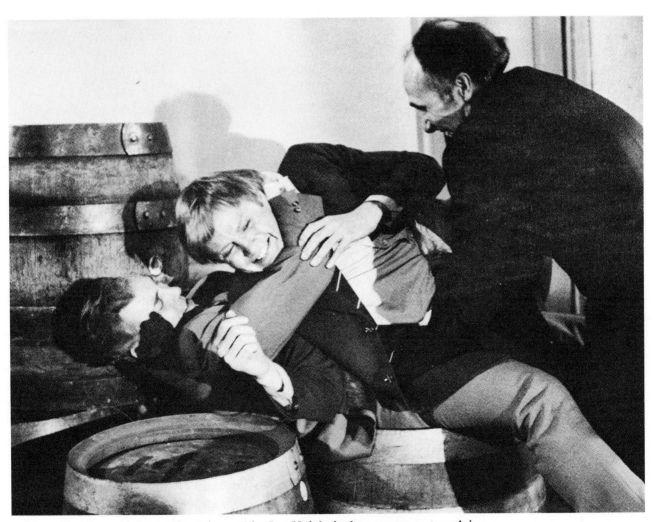

The Odessa File. Jon Voight is the newsman at work in this lively melodrama about a secret Nazi organization he sought to uncover. (Columbia, 1974)

The Parallax View. Warren Beatty played an overly curious newsman in this chilling examination of assassination conspiracies in general. (Paramount, 1974)

Parallax View, in which reporter Warren Beatty began investigating the possibility of an assassination conspiracy and ended up being trapped by the conspirators. Suggested by the political assassinations of the 1960s, the film played effectively on the public's possibly paranoid fear of an organized conspiracy behind every political killing. But despite the visual and suspenseful plusses in Pakula's chilling movie, there was a serious minus: it fell into the oldest of Hollywood cliché traps, the one which calls for the newsman to infiltrate the ranks of the Bad Guys, losing sight of his role as a reporter rather than as an avenger. But at least Pakula had the courage to dispense with the traditional happy ending.

Also in 1974, television made a couple of attempts at reintroducing the newspaperman to the home audience. One was called "No. 19 Coronado Drive," and it had Fred MacMurray as the owner of a newspaper, but in keeping with the clichés of television situation comedy, MacMurray had a large and vocal family. The ninety-minute program, intended as a pilot for a series, slipped quietly into obscurity after its initial airing.

And Darren McGavin (who had starred in the "Crime Photographer" series back in the early 1950s) was cast as a reporter in an ABC series called "The Night Stalker." This had first been tested as a television movie with the same title, and it was regarded as successful enough to lead, first, to a sequel called *The Night Strangler* and then to the series, reverting to the original title.

Typical of television's endless searching for "originality," Carl Kolchak, the reporter played by McGavin, kept tripping over stories involving werewolves, vampires, and other such unlikely creatures. And by way of giving Kolchak still more scope, the reporter, who had originally worked for a Seattle newspaper, was now employed by a second-rate wire service, based in Chicago, but now able to roam from city to city in quest of these eerie yarns.

So much for television's interest in the realities of the press, circa 1974.

Looking back on some forty years of newspaper movies, it's debatable whether the reporter has made much progress on the screen. Whatever sophistication he may have acquired, whatever shifts the public's comprehension of him may have experienced, whatever range of "types" he has represented, and whatever difference in the degree of faith the public may have in his integrity, he really isn't so very different from those two attractively imperfect newsmen created by Ben Hecht and Charles MacArthur back in 1928, which may be another way of saying that public taste in popular movies hasn't changed all that much, either.

The newspaper reporter today is a far less frequent character on movie screens, partly because police, private eyes, espionage agents, and western lawmen have demonstrated more staying power as acceptable popular heroes—and partly, too, because the newspaper is no longer perceived as being the vital force it was thirty or forty years ago.

But for most of the years since talking pictures were introduced, the gentlemen and ladies of the press have entertained millions of people with wit, daring, irreverence, roguery, omniscience, charm, and gusto.

And they aren't quite ready to write "30" yet.

INDEX